THE COMPLETE KETO DIET COOKBOOK

Easy, Delicious Recipes to Fuel Your Ketogenic Lifestyle and Support Healthy Living | Full Color Edition

Christina J. Williamson

Manufactured in the United States of America
Interior and Cover Designer: Danielle Rees
Art Producer: Brooke White
Editor: Aaliyah Lyons
Production Editor: Sienna Adams
Production Manager: Sarah Johnson
Photography: Michael Smith

TABLE OF CONTENTS

TABLE OF CONTENTS

TABLE OF CONTENTS

INTRODUCTION

When I first decided to try the keto diet, it was all about getting in better shape. I was tired of feeling sluggish and just wasn't seeing the fitness results I wanted from my regular routine. I knew I had to make a change, but I didn't expect keto to be the game-changer it turned out to be. The idea of cutting carbs seemed daunting at first, but once I dove in, I found it surprisingly manageable—and it worked. I started shedding those extra pounds, felt more energized, and was finally able to see real muscle definition that I had been working so hard for.

What really kept me going, though, was the support I got from friends who were on the same journey. They shared their struggles, recipes, and tips, which made everything feel less intimidating. Soon, we were swapping keto-friendly dishes like they were going out of style. The more I stuck with it, the more I collected new recipes, tweaks, and insights that helped me stay on track. Now, I'm excited to share all of this with you, hoping it helps others just like it helped me—transforming not just my body, but my relationship with food.

DEDICATION

To Louis, I can't thank you enough for everything you've done for me. From the moment we met at the gym, you've been there, guiding me through the ups and downs of the keto diet. Your experience, encouragement, and practical advice have been invaluable in helping me reach a place I never thought possible. What I've accomplished today, both in fitness and with my diet, would never have happened without you by my side. You've truly made all the difference, and I'll always be grateful for your friendship and support. Thank you from the bottom of my heart.

1

CHAPTER 1: SMOOTH SAILING ON KETO

WHAT IS THE KETO DIET?

The keto diet is a high-fat, low-carb way of eating that's all about getting your body into a state called ketosis. Instead of relying on carbs for energy, your body switches over to burning fat for fuel. Basically, when you eat fewer carbs, your body runs out of glucose (the sugar from carbs) to burn and starts breaking down fat into ketones. These ketones then become the new energy source for your body and brain.

Overview of the Ketogenic Diet At its core, the keto diet is about cutting back on carbs and loading up on fats. You're looking at eating around 70% fat, 25% protein, and only 5% carbs. This drastic carb reduction is what helps your body enter ketosis. You'll be eating mostly healthy fats like avocados, olive oil, and nuts, along with moderate amounts of protein from foods like meat, fish, and eggs. Veggies like leafy greens and cauliflower are your best friends, while bread, pasta, and sugary snacks are a no-go.

The goal is to retrain your body to use fat as fuel instead of carbs, which leads to some pretty interesting results. It's not about cutting calories—it's about changing how your body processes food.

The Science Behind Ketosis So, how does ketosis work? Normally, your body burns glucose (from carbs) for energy. But when carbs are limited, your liver breaks down fats into ketones. These ketones then become your body's primary energy source. It's a pretty cool metabolic shift that gives your body a new way to burn fat, and it doesn't happen overnight. It usually takes a few days for your body to adjust, which is why some people experience something called the "keto flu" at the start. It's temporary—headaches, tiredness, and mood swings—but once your body adapts, you'll be burning fat like a pro.

Benefits of the Keto Diet The keto diet has some serious perks that go beyond just weight loss. Here's why so many people are jumping on the keto bandwagon:

- **Weight Loss** One of the biggest reasons people try keto is for weight loss. Since your body is burning fat for fuel, you'll start to shed the extra pounds. Plus, the keto diet has a natural appetite-suppressing effect, which means you're less likely to overeat. You'll feel fuller for longer, and fat burns slower than carbs, which means steady, consistent energy throughout the day.

- **Increased Energy** Once your body adapts to using fat as fuel, many people say they feel more energized and less sluggish. Unlike carbs, which can cause energy spikes followed by crashes, fat provides a steady, reliable source of energy. This means no more mid-afternoon slumps!

- **Improved Mental Clarity** Another big bonus of the keto diet is improved focus. Ketones are a much cleaner energy source for your brain than glucose, so you may notice better concentration and mental clarity. No more brain fog—just clear thinking all day long.

HOW TO START THE KETO DIET

Starting the keto diet might sound a little tricky at first, but once you get the hang of it, it's pretty straightforward. The key is understanding the basics and making gradual changes so your body can adjust. Let's break it down step-by-step so you can dive in with confidence.

Understand Macronutrient Ratios One of the first things you'll need to get used to on the keto diet is the breakdown of macronutrients (fats, proteins, and carbs). The idea is to shift your food choices so that about 70% of your calories come from fats, 25% from protein, and only 5% from carbs. This might sound like a lot of fat, but don't worry—healthy fats are your new best friend.

Fats help keep you full and give you steady energy throughout the day, so don't shy away from foods like avocados, olive oil, coconut oil, and fatty cuts of meat. Protein is important for muscle maintenance and overall health, but you don't need to overdo it. Too much protein can kick you out of ketosis, so keep it moderate. When it comes to carbs, you'll want to keep them as low as possible—around 20-30 grams of net carbs per day is the goal for most people on keto. Focus on non-starchy vegetables, like leafy greens, zucchini, and cauliflower, to meet your carb needs.

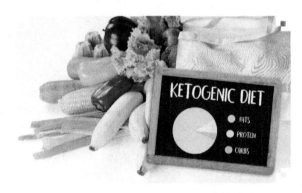

Gradually Reduce Carbs One of the most common challenges people face when starting keto is the so-called "keto flu." This happens when your body is adjusting from burning carbs for fuel to burning fat. It's like a transition period where you might feel tired, moody, or headachy. But don't worry—it's temporary.

To minimize the effects of the keto flu, the key is to ease into the diet. Rather than drastically cutting carbs right away, try reducing them gradually over a week or two. This way, your body has time to adjust without going through major withdrawal. Start by cutting out the obvious carbs—like bread, pasta, and sugary foods—and replace them with low-carb options. You don't have to be perfect from day one, just aim to reduce your carb intake each day. This gradual approach helps prevent those unpleasant side effects and sets you up for long-term success.

Starting the keto diet doesn't have to be overwhelming. Focus on getting the right balance of macronutrients, gradually cutting carbs, and stocking up on the right foods. Before you know it, you'll be on your way to reaching your goals and feeling great. Just take it one step at a time, and don't stress about being perfect. Keto is all about making lasting, sustainable changes to your eating habits!

COMMON CHALLENGES AND HOW TO OVERCOME THEM

Starting the keto diet can feel like a breeze at first, but over time, you'll likely encounter a few challenges. It's totally normal, and the good news is that you can overcome these hurdles with the right mindset and preparation. Let's talk about some of the most common challenges people face on keto and how to handle them without feeling overwhelmed.

Navigating Social Situations One of the toughest parts of starting any diet is dealing with social situations—whether it's eating out at a restaurant, attending family gatherings, or going to parties. You may find yourself surrounded by carb-heavy foods like pizza, pasta, and cake, and it can be tempting to indulge. But don't worry; it's possible to navigate these situations while staying true to your keto goals.

When dining out, check the menu ahead of time and look for options that can be modified to fit your keto needs. For example, you can ask for a burger without the bun, replace fries with a side salad, or opt for grilled fish with veggies instead of starchy sides. Many restaurants are accommodating when you ask for substitutions, so don't be shy to ask.

At family gatherings or parties, bring your own keto-friendly dish to share. This way, you'll have something safe to eat, and you can even introduce others to some delicious keto recipes. If you're attending a BBQ, for example, bring a keto-friendly dip or a side salad with avocado and bacon. And remember, it's okay to politely decline foods that don't fit your diet—focus on enjoying the conversation and the company, not the food.

Dealing with the "Keto Flu" When you first start keto, you might experience some temporary side effects collectively known as the "keto flu." This can include headaches, fatigue, irritability, and muscle cramps as your body adjusts to burning fat instead of carbs. It's completely normal, but it can be uncomfortable if you're not prepared.

The best way to deal with keto flu is to ease into the diet gradually. Reducing carbs slowly, as mentioned earlier, helps your body adjust without a shock to the system. But if you're already feeling the symptoms, there are a few remedies that can help:

Stay Hydrated: As your body shifts to burning fat, you'll lose water weight, which can lead to dehydration. Drink plenty of water throughout the day, and consider adding electrolytes (like sodium, potassium, and magnesium) to replenish what your body may be losing.

Increase Salt Intake: Keto reduces your body's insulin levels, which in turn causes your kidneys to excrete more sodium. This can lead to low salt levels, so don't be afraid to add a pinch of salt to your meals or drink bone broth to help replenish electrolytes.

Eat More Fat: If you're feeling sluggish, you might not be eating enough fat. Remember, fat is your main fuel on keto, so make sure you're getting enough—whether it's through avocado, nuts, or coconut oil.

Most of the keto flu symptoms will subside after a few days, but these tips can help speed up the adjustment period.

Staying Motivated Staying motivated on the keto diet—especially after the initial excitement wears off—can be tough. But there are a few strategies to keep you going and make sure you stick with the lifestyle for the long haul.

- **Set Realistic Goals:** Setting small, achievable goals will give you something to work toward and help you feel accomplished along the way. Whether it's sticking to your daily carb limit or hitting a weight loss milestone, celebrating those small victories keeps you motivated.

- **Track Your Progress:** It's easy to get discouraged if you're not seeing immediate results. Try tracking your meals, progress photos, or even how you feel each day. You might not see major changes every day, but over time, you'll notice improvements in energy levels, mental clarity, and weight loss.

- **Find Support:** One of the best ways to stay motivated is to surround yourself with others who are on the same journey. Whether it's joining an online keto group, asking friends to go keto with you, or finding a workout buddy who supports your goals, having people who understand and encourage you makes a huge difference.

FOODS TO AVOID & FOODS TO ENJOY

KETO FOODS TO AVOID
LOW FAT / HIGH CARB (BASED ON NET CARBS)

MEATS & MEAT ALTERNATIVES
- Deli meat (some, not all)
- Hot dogs (with fillers)
- Sausage (with fillers)
- Seitan
- Tofu

DAIRY
- Almond milk (sweetened)
- Coconut milk (sweetened)
- Milk
- Soy milk (regular)
- Yogurt (regular)

NUTS & SEEDS
- Cashews
- Chestnuts
- Pistachios

VEGETABLES
- Artichokes
- Beans (all varieties)
- Burdock root
- Butternut squash
- Chickpeas
- Corn
- Edamame
- Eggplant
- Leeks
- Parsnips
- Plantains
- Potatoes
- Sweet potatoes
- Taro root
- Turnips
- Winter squash
- Yams

FRUITS &
- Apples
- Apricots
- Bananas
- Boysenberries
- Cantaloupe
- Cherries
- Currants
- Dates
- Elderberries
- Gooseberries
- Grapes
- Honeydew melon
- Huckleberries
- Kiwifruits
- Mangos
- Oranges
- Peaches
- Peas
- Pineapples
- Plums
- Prunes
- Raisins
- Water chestnuts

KETO COOKING STAPLES

1. Pink Himalayan salt
2. Freshly ground black pepper
3. Ghee (clarified butter, without dairy; buy grass-fed if you can)
4. Olive oil
5. Grass-fed butter

KETO PERISHABLES

1. Eggs (pasture-raised, if you can)
2. Avocados
3. Bacon (uncured)
4. Cream cheese (full-fat; or use a dairy-free alternative)
5. Sour cream (full-fat; or use a dairy-free alternative)
6. Heavy whipping cream or coconut milk (full-fat; I buy the coconut milk in a can)
7. Garlic (fresh or pre-minced in a jar)
8. Cauliflower
9. Meat (grass-fed, if you can)
10. Greens (spinach, kale, or arugula)

KETO FOODS TO ENJOY
HIGH FAT / LOW CARB (BASED ON NET CARBS)

MEATS & SEAFOOD
- Beef (ground beef, steak, etc.)
- Chicken
- Crab
- Crawfish
- Duck
- Fish
- Goose
- Lamb
- Lobster
- Mussels
- Octopus
- Pork (pork chops, bacon, etc.)
- Quail
- Sausage (without fillers)
- Scallops
- Shrimp
- Veal
- Venison

DAIRY
- Blue cheese dressing
- Burrata cheese
- Cottage cheese
- Cream cheese
- Eggs
- Greek yogurt (full-fat)
- Grilling cheese
- Halloumi cheese
- Heavy (whipping) cream
- Homemade whipped cream
- Kefalotyri cheese
- Mozzarella cheese
- Provolone cheese
- Queso blanco
- Ranch dressing
- Ricotta cheese
- Unsweetened almond milk
- Unsweetened coconut milk

VEGETABLES
- Alfalfa sprouts
- Asparagus
- Avocados
- Bell peppers
- Broccoli
- Cabbage
- Carrots (in moderation)
- Cauliflower
- Celery
- Chicory
- Coconut
- Cucumbers
- Garlic (in moderation)
- Green beans
- Herbs
- Jicama
- Lemons
- Limes
- Mushrooms
- Okra
- Olives
- Onions (in moderation)
- Pickles
- Pumpkin
- Radishes
- Salad greens
- Scallions
- Spaghetti squash (in moderation)
- Tomatoes (in moderation)
- Zucchini

NUTS & SEEDS
- Almonds
- Brazil nuts
- Chia seeds
- Flaxseeds
- Hazelnuts
- Macadamia nuts
- Peanuts (in moderation)
- Pecans
- Pine nuts
- Pumpkin seeds
- Sacha inchi seeds
- Sesame seeds
- Walnuts

FRUITS
- Blackberries
- Blueberries
- Cranberries
- Raspberries
- Strawberries

CHAPTER 2: 4-WEEK MEAL PLAN

WEEK 1

Day 1:

Breakfast: Almond Butter Smoothie

Lunch: Turkish Chicken Kebabs

Snack: Flourless Chocolate Hazelnut Brownie Pie (2 Serves)

Dinner: Classic Cobb Salad

Total for the day:

Calories: 2012; Fat: 156g; Carbs: 42.6g; Fiber: 21.5g; Protein: 112.6g

Day 2:

Breakfast: Keto Waffles

Lunch: Easy Jerk Ribs

Snack: Flourless Chocolate Hazelnut Brownie Pie (2 Serves)

Dinner: Cauliflower Lobster Risotto

Total for the day:

Calories: 1914; Fat: 146.5g; Carbs: 34.3g; Fiber: 13.6g; Protein: 109.4g

Day 3:

Breakfast: Mediterranean Scrambled Eggs

Lunch: Turkish Chicken Kebabs

Snack: Fresh Berry Mascarpone Tart (2 Serves)

Dinner: Classic Cobb Salad

Total for the day:

Calories: 1801; Fat: 123.9g; Carbs: 30.4g; Fiber: 13.3g; Protein: 119.8g

Day 4:

Breakfast: Almond Butter Smoothie

Lunch: Easy Jerk Ribs

Snack: Fresh Berry Mascarpone Tart (2 Serves)

Dinner: Cauliflower Lobster Risotto

Total for the day:

Calories: 1855; Fat: 142.4g; Carbs: 45.2g; Fiber: 18.6g; Protein: 84g

Day 5:

Breakfast: Mediterranean Scrambled Eggs

Lunch: Easy Jerk Ribs

Snack: Fresh Berry Mascarpone Tart (2 Serves)

Dinner: Classic Cobb Salad

Total for the day:

Calories: 1693; Fat: 127.7g; Carbs: 30.2g; Fiber: 13.8g; Protein: 85.8g

Day 6:

Breakfast: Keto Waffles

Lunch: Fish Taco Bowl

Snack: Flourless Chocolate Hazelnut Brownie Pie (2 Serves)

Dinner: Cauliflower Lobster Risotto

Total for the day:

Calories: 1849; Fat: 143.5g; Carbs: 40.3g; Fiber: 18.6g; Protein: 99.4g

Day 7:

Breakfast: Mediterranean Scrambled Eggs

Lunch: Fish Taco Bowl

Snack: Flourless Chocolate Hazelnut Brownie Pie (2 Serves)

Dinner: Classic Cobb Salad

Total for the day:

Calories: 1696; Fat: 139.1g; Carbs: 34.6g; Fiber: 20g; Protein: 79.4g

WEEK 2

Day 1:

Breakfast: Bacon and Egg Muffins

Lunch: Pork and Sausage Endive Wraps

Snack: Chocolate Almond Keto Cookies (2 Serves)

Dinner: Pan-Seared Salmon with Braised Kale

Total for the day:

Calories: 1981; Fat: 149.1g; Carbs: 37.1g; Fiber: 20.5g; Protein: 112.5g

Day 2:

Breakfast: Keto Breakfast Casserole

Lunch: Pork and Sausage Endive Wraps

Snack: Hot Artichoke and Cheese Dip (2 Serves)

Dinner: Classic Egg Salad

Total for the day:

Calories: 1935; Fat: 177g; Carbs: 30.2g; Fiber: 11g; Protein: 112.8g

Day 3:

Breakfast: Coconut Chai Vanilla Smoothie

Lunch: Spanish-Style Stuffed Peppers

Snack: Chocolate Almond Keto Cookies (2 Serves)

Dinner: Pan-Seared Salmon with Braised Kale

Total for the day:

Calories: 1848; Fat: 136.2g; Carbs: 38.3g; Fiber: 19.8g; Protein: 99.0g

Day 4:

Breakfast: Keto Breakfast Casserole

Lunch: Pork and Sausage Endive Wraps

Snack: Hot Artichoke and Cheese Dip (2 Serves)

Dinner: Spanish-Style Stuffed Peppers

Total for the day:

Calories: 1907; Fat: 149.7g; Carbs: 25.4g; Fiber: 10.5g; Protein: 105.3g

Day 5:

Breakfast: Bacon and Egg Muffins

Lunch: Classic Egg Salad

Snack: Chocolate Almond Keto Cookies (2 Serves)

Dinner: Pan-Seared Salmon with Braised Kale

Total for the day:

Calories: 1946; Fat: 154.2g; Carbs: 36.6g; Fiber: 18.3g; Protein: 93.9g

Day 6:

Breakfast: Bacon and Egg Muffins

Lunch: Spanish-Style Stuffed Peppers

Snack: Hot Artichoke and Cheese Dip (2 Serves)

Dinner: Pan-Seared Salmon with Braised Kale

Total for the day:

Calories: 1722; Fat: 142.6g; Carbs: 26.5g; Fiber: 9.6g; Protein: 85.4g

Day 7:

Breakfast: Keto Breakfast Casserole

Lunch: Pork and Sausage Endive Wraps

Snack: Chocolate Almond Keto Cookies (2 Serves)

Dinner: Spanish-Style Stuffed Peppers

Total for the day:

Calories: 2043; Fat: 154.3g; Carbs: 35.2g; Fiber: 19.7g; Protein: 112.9g

WEEK 3

Day 1:

Breakfast: **Chewy Keto Bagels**

Lunch: **Shredded Beef with Herbs**

Snack: **Peanut Butter Caramel Cookies (2 Serves)**

Dinner: **Texas-Style Keto Chili**

Total for the day:

Calories: 1755; Fat: 109.2g; Carbs: 27.6g; Fiber: 8.5g; Protein: 81.4g

Day 2:

Breakfast: **Sausage & Egg–Stuffed Portobello Mushrooms**

Lunch: **Shredded Beef with Herbs**

Snack: **Peanut Butter Caramel Cookies (2 Serves)**

Dinner: **Texas-Style Keto Chili**

Total for the day:

Calories: 1930; Fat: 130.9g; Carbs: 25.6g; Fiber: 6.9g; Protein: 95.3g

Day 3:

Breakfast: **Chewy Keto Bagels**

Lunch: **Tuna, Avocado and Ham Wraps**

Snack: **Basic Almond Flour Muffins**

Dinner: **Texas-Style Keto Chili**

Total for the day:

Calories: 1768; Fat: 100.4g; Carbs: 26.8g; Fiber: 11.6g; Protein: 91.1g

Day 4:

Breakfast: **Sausage & Egg–Stuffed Portobello Mushrooms**

Lunch: **Tuna, Avocado and Ham Wraps**

Snack: **Peanut Butter Caramel Cookies**

Dinner: **Chilled Shrimp and Avocado Salad**

Total for the day:

Calories: 1760; Fat: 111.5g; Carbs: 20.9g; Fiber: 10.2g; Protein: 111.1g

Day 5:

Breakfast: **Chewy Keto Bagels**

Lunch: **Shredded Beef with Herbs**

Snack: **Basic Almond Flour Muffins (2 Serves)**

Dinner: **Chilled Shrimp and Avocado Salad**

Total for the day:

Calories: 1940; Fat: 129.2g; Carbs: 30.4g; Fiber: 13.6g; Protein: 99g

Day 6:

Breakfast: **Sausage & Egg–Stuffed Portobello Mushrooms**

Lunch: **Tuna, Avocado and Ham Wraps**

Snack: **Basic Almond Flour Muffins**

Dinner: **Chilled Shrimp and Avocado Salad**

Total for the day:

Calories: 1773; Fat: 115g; Carbs: 21.3g; Fiber: 11g; Protein: 111.9g

Day 7:

Breakfast: **Chewy Keto Bagels**

Lunch: **Shredded Beef with Herbs**

Snack: **Peanut Butter Caramel Cookies (2 Serves)**

Dinner: **Texas-Style Keto Chili**

Total for the day:

Calories: 1755; Fat: 109.2g; Carbs: 27.6g; Fiber: 8.5g; Protein: 81.4g

WEEK 4

Day 1:

Breakfast: **Avocado Smoothie**

Lunch: **Buffalo Chicken Wings**

Snack: **Crustless Coconut Custard Pie (2 Serves)**

Dinner: **Zucchini Lasagna**

Total for the day:

Calories: 2015; Fat: 145.5g; Carbs: 28.3g; Fiber: 12.5g; Protein: 65.0g

Day 2:

Breakfast: **Bacon and Roasted Pepper Deviled Eggs**

Lunch: **Buffalo Chicken Wings**

Snack: **Crustless Coconut Custard Pie (2 Serves)**

Dinner: **Zucchini Lasagna**

Total for the day:

Calories: 1978; Fat: 137.8g; Carbs: 26.1g; Fiber: 8.3g; Protein: 79.6g

Day 3:

Breakfast: **Avocado Smoothie**

Lunch: **Green Chicken Curry**

Snack: **Cream Cheese Biscuits (2 Serves)**

Dinner: **Zucchini Lasagna**

Total for the day:

Calories: 1811; Fat: 125g; Carbs: 33.2g; Fiber: 15.2g; Protein: 79.2g

Day 4:

Breakfast: **Bacon and Roasted Pepper Deviled Eggs**

Lunch: **Green Chicken Curry**

Snack: **Cream Cheese Biscuits (2 Serves)**

Dinner: **Shrimp Caprese Salad**

Total for the day:

Calories: 1765; Fat: 117.3g; Carbs: 27g; Fiber: 10g; Protein: 92.8g

Day 5:

Breakfast: **Coconut Chai Vanilla Smoothie**

Lunch: **Broccoli Slaw with Tahini Dressing**

Snack: **Crustless Coconut Custard Pie (2 Serves)**

Dinner: **Zucchini Lasagna**

Total for the day:

Calories: 1888; Fat: 120.3g; Carbs: 31.2g; Fiber: 11.7g; Protein: 75.3g

Day 6:

Breakfast: **Bacon and Roasted Pepper Deviled Eggs**

Lunch: **Green Chicken Curry**

Snack: **Cream Cheese Biscuits (2 Serves)**

Dinner: **Shrimp Caprese Salad**

Total for the day:

Calories: 1765; Fat: 117.3g; Carbs: 27g; Fiber: 10g; Protein: 92.8g

Day 7:

Breakfast: **Bacon and Roasted Pepper Deviled Eggs**

Lunch: **Broccoli Slaw with Tahini Dressing**

Snack: **Crustless Coconut Custard Pie (2 Serves)**

Dinner: **Shrimp Caprese Salad**

Total for the day:

Calories: 1941; Fat: 133.6g; Carbs: 28.0g; Fiber: 10.4g; Protein: 79.9g

CHAPTER 3: BREAKFAST AND SMOOTHIES

CHEWY KETO BAGELS

Prep time: 20 minutes | **Cook time: 20 minutes** | **Serves 8**

Everything Bagel Topping:
- 1 teaspoon white sesame seeds
- 1 teaspoon poppy seeds
- 1 teaspoon dried minced onion
- ½ teaspoon coarse sea salt
- Optional: 1 teaspoon dried garlic flakes

Bagels:
- 1 recipe nut-free magic mozzarella dough
- 1 tablespoon unsalted butter, melted
- 1 large egg, beaten (for egg wash, optional for better browning)

1. Preheat the oven to 350°F. Line a large baking sheet with parchment paper or a silicone baking mat.
2. In a small shallow bowl, combine sesame seeds, poppy seeds, dried minced onion, and sea salt. If using, add dried garlic flakes. Set aside.
3. Prepare the magic mozzarella dough according to recipe directions.
4. Divide the prepared dough into 8 equal portions (about 2½ ounces each for consistency). Roll each portion into a log approximately 8 inches long and ½ inch thick.
5. Form each log into a circle by pinching the ends together firmly to seal. Place formed bagels on the prepared baking sheet, leaving about 2 inches between each.
6. Brush the tops and sides of each bagel with melted butter (or egg wash if using). Press the top side firmly into the seed mixture to coat well.
7. Bake for 15-20 minutes, or until bagels are puffed up and golden brown. The internal temperature should reach 190°F when tested with a food thermometer.
8. Let cool on the baking sheet for 5 minutes, then transfer to a wire rack to cool completely.

Per Serving

Calories: **290** | Fat: **12.3g** | Carbs: **5.5g** | Fiber: **2.6g** | Protein: **12.1g**

BERRY SMOOTHIE

Prep time: 5 minutes | **Cook time: 0 minutes** | **Serves 2**

- ½ cup mixed berries (blueberries, raspberries, strawberries)
- ½ cup unsweetened almond milk
- ¼ cup heavy cream
- 1 tablespoon chia seeds
- 1 tablespoon erythritol (or sweetener of choice)
- Ice cubes (optional)

1. In a blender, combine the mixed berries, almond milk, heavy cream, chia seeds, and sweetener.
2. Blend until smooth. If desired, add ice cubes and blend again for a thicker smoothie.
3. Pour into glasses and serve immediately.

Per Serving

Calories: **180** | Fat: **16g** | Carbs: **6g** | Fiber: **3g** | Protein: **2g**

BACON AND EGG MUFFINS

Prep time: **10 minutes** | Cook time: **20 minutes** | Serves **6**

- 6 large eggs
- ½ cup cooked bacon, chopped
- ¼ cup heavy cream
- ¼ cup shredded mozzarella cheese
- ¼ teaspoon garlic powder
- Salt and pepper, to taste
- Fresh herbs (optional, for garnish)

1. Preheat the oven to 350°F and grease a muffin tin with cooking spray.
2. In a mixing bowl, whisk together the eggs, heavy cream, garlic powder, salt, and pepper.
3. Divide the chopped bacon evenly among the muffin cups.
4. Pour the egg mixture over the bacon and sprinkle with shredded mozzarella cheese.
5. Bake for 15–20 minutes, or until the muffins are set and lightly golden on top.
6. Let cool for a few minutes before removing from the muffin tin. Garnish with fresh herbs if desired.

Per Serving

Calories: **210** | Fat: **18g** | Carbs: **2g** | Fiber: **0g** | Protein: **13g**

EGG-IN-A-HOLE BREAKFAST BURGER

Prep time: **5 minutes** | Cook time: **15 minutes** | Serves **2**

- 4 slices bacon
- 6 ounces ground beef
- Pink Himalayan salt
- Freshly ground black pepper
- 2 tablespoons butter
- 2 large eggs
- 2 slices Cheddar cheese
- 1 tablespoon Sriracha mayo

1. In a large skillet over medium-high heat, cook the bacon on both sides until crispy, about 8 minutes. Transfer the bacon to a paper towel-lined plate.
2. Form the ground beef into two burger patties. Use a small glass or cookie cutter to cut out the center of each patty (like a donut). Take the cut-out meat and add it to the edges of the two patties. Season with pink Himalayan salt and pepper.
3. In the same skillet, melt the butter over medium-high heat. Add the burger patties, cooking the first side for 2 minutes before flipping.
4. Crack one egg into the center of each patty. Cook until the whites are set, 1 to 2 minutes. Season the eggs with salt and pepper.
5. Place a slice of Cheddar cheese on top of each egg. Turn off the heat and cover the skillet to melt the cheese, about 2 minutes.
6. Transfer the burgers to two plates. Top each with two slices of bacon and a dollop of Sriracha mayo. Serve immediately.

Per Serving

Calories: **578** | Total Fat: **48g** | Carbs: **2g** | Net Carbs: **2g** | Fiber: **0g** | Protein: **34g**

ALMOND BUTTER SMOOTHIE

Prep time: **5 minutes** | Cook time: **5 minutes** | Serves **2**

- 1 cup unsweetened full-fat coconut milk (from a can, not coconut milk beverage)
- 1 scoop chocolate sea salt flavored keto exogenous ketone powder (about 0.8 oz)
- ½ medium ripe avocado (about 2.5 oz)
- 2 tablespoons creamy almond butter
- ½ cup mixed berries, fresh or frozen (no sugar added)
- ½ cup ice cubes (about 4-5 standard cubes)
- ¼ teaspoon liquid stevia, or to taste (optional)

1. Add ingredients to a high-powered blender in this order: coconut milk, ketone powder, avocado, almond butter, berries, and ice.
2. Blend on high speed for 45-60 seconds or until completely smooth and creamy. Stop and scrape down sides if needed.
3. Taste and add stevia if desired, blending briefly to incorporate.
4. Pour immediately into two 12-ounce glasses and serve.

Per Serving

Calories: **446** | Fat: **43g** | Carbs: **16g** | Fiber: **7g** | Protein: **7g**

KETO WAFFLES

Prep time: **5 minutes** | Cook time: **10 minutes** | Serves **2**

- 2 large eggs
- 1 tablespoon unsweetened vanilla almond milk
- 1 teaspoon vanilla extract
- 1 scoop vanilla keto protein powder
- 1 teaspoon baking powder
- Pinch of sea salt
- 1 tablespoon butter
- ½ teaspoon cinnamon

1. Preheat a waffle maker and lightly spray with nonstick spray.
2. In a mixing bowl, whisk together the eggs, almond milk, and vanilla extract until bubbly.
3. Add the protein powder, baking powder, and salt to the mixture. Whisk until smooth.
4. Pour ¼ cup of batter onto the preheated waffle maker. Cook until golden brown, then remove to a plate. Repeat with the remaining batter.
5. Spread butter over the waffles and sprinkle with cinnamon.

Per Serving

Calories: **437** | Fat: **32.7g** | Protein: **27.8g** | Carbs: **6.7g** | Fiber: **0.8g**

SAUSAGE & EGG–STUFFED PORTOBELLO MUSHROOMS

Prep time: 8 minutes | Cook time: 27 minutes | Serves 4

- 4 large portobello mushroom caps
- Kosher salt and freshly ground black pepper
- 1 pound bulk country-style breakfast sausage
- 4 large eggs
- 1 tablespoon fresh parsley, chopped, for garnish

1. Preheat the oven to 375°F. Remove the stems from the mushroom caps and scrape out the gills with a spoon. Season the caps with salt and pepper.
2. Divide the sausage into 4 equal portions. Press a portion of the sausage along the bottom and up the sides of each mushroom cap to form a cup for the egg. Place the sausage-stuffed mushrooms on a baking sheet and bake for 15 minutes.
3. Remove the mushroom caps from the oven and blot any liquid from the centers. Crack an egg into each mushroom cap. Return to the oven and bake for 12 more minutes for firm whites and slightly runny yolks. If you prefer hard yolks, increase the cooking time to 15 minutes, or until the eggs are cooked to your liking.
4. Serve hot or at room temperature, garnished with fresh parsley.
5. Store in an airtight container in the refrigerator for up to 3 days. To reheat, microwave on high for 30 seconds.

Per Serving

Calories: 465 | Fat: 34g | Protein: 26g | Carbs: 3.5g | Fiber: 1g

AVOCADO SMOOTHIE

Prep time: 5 minutes | Cook time: 0 minutes | Serves 2

- 1 ripe avocado, peeled and pitted
- ½ cup unsweetened almond milk
- ¼ cup heavy cream
- 1 tablespoon chia seeds
- 1 teaspoon vanilla extract
- 1–2 tablespoons erythritol (or sweetener of choice)
- Ice cubes (optional)

1. In a blender, combine the avocado, almond milk, heavy cream, chia seeds, vanilla extract, and sweetener.
2. Blend until smooth and creamy. Add ice cubes and blend again if you prefer a thicker, colder smoothie.
3. Pour into glasses and serve immediately.

Per Serving

Calories: 330 | Fat: 30g | Carbs: 7g | Fiber: 5g | Protein: 4g

MEDITERRANEAN SCRAMBLED EGGS

Prep time: **5 minutes** | Cook time: **10 minutes** |Serves **3**

- 2 tablespoons unsalted butter
- 4 tablespoons plain Greek yogurt
- 6 large eggs
- ½ teaspoon cayenne pepper
- ½ teaspoon dried oregano
- ½ teaspoon dried basil
- Sea salt and freshly ground black pepper, to taste
- 3 ounces halloumi cheese, crumbled (about ¾ cup)

1. Melt the butter in a large nonstick skillet over medium heat.
2. In a medium bowl, whisk together the Greek yogurt, eggs, cayenne pepper, oregano, basil, salt, and black pepper until well combined.
3. Pour the yogurt-egg mixture into the skillet. Cook, stirring frequently with a rubber spatula, for about 6 minutes or until eggs form thick and creamy curds.
4. Top with crumbled halloumi cheese and serve warm.

Per Serving

Calories: **313** | Fat: **25.3g** | Carbs: **2g** | Protein: **18.8g** | Fiber: **0.2g**

KETO BREAKFAST CASSEROLE

Prep time: **15 minutes** | Cook time: **45 minutes** | Serves **6**

- 1 tablespoon olive oil
- ½ pound breakfast sausage
- 1 small onion, diced
- 1 bell pepper, diced
- 6 large eggs
- ½ cup heavy cream
- ½ teaspoon garlic powder
- ½ teaspoon paprika
- 1 cup shredded Cheddar cheese
- Salt and pepper, to taste

1. Preheat the oven to 375°F and grease a 9x9 baking dish with olive oil.
2. In a skillet, cook the breakfast sausage over medium heat until browned. Remove from heat and set aside.
3. In the same skillet, sauté the onion and bell pepper until softened, about 5 minutes.
4. In a mixing bowl, whisk together the eggs, heavy cream, garlic powder, paprika, salt, and pepper.
5. Layer the cooked sausage, onions, and bell peppers in the prepared baking dish. Pour the egg mixture over the top.
6. Sprinkle the shredded Cheddar cheese on top and bake for 35–45 minutes, or until set and golden brown on top.
7. Let cool for 5 minutes before slicing.

Per Serving

Calories: **370** | Fat: **29g** | Carbs: **4g** | Fiber: **1g** | Protein: **25g**

COCONUT CHAI VANILLA SMOOTHIE

Prep time: 5 minutes | Cook time: 15 minutes | Serves 1

- ½ cup brewed chai tea, cooled to room temperature
- ½ cup unsweetened vanilla almond milk
- 2 tablespoons full-fat unsweetened coconut milk (from can)
- 2 tablespoons sugar-free vanilla protein powder
- 1 tablespoon granulated erythritol, or to taste
- ¼ teaspoon pure vanilla extract
- ⅛ teaspoon ground cinnamon, plus more for garnish
- 3 ice cubes

1. Place the chai tea, almond milk, coconut milk, protein powder, erythritol, vanilla extract, cinnamon, and ice cubes in a blender.
2. Blend until smooth and creamy, about 30-45 seconds.
3. Taste and adjust sweetness with additional erythritol if desired.
4. Pour into a 12-ounce glass and garnish with a light dusting of cinnamon, if desired. Serve immediately.

Per Serving

Calories:231 | Fat: 8g | Protein: 18g | Carbs: 4g | Fiber: 1g

BACON AND ROASTED PEPPER DEVILED EGGS

Prep time: 15 minutes | Cook time: 20 minutes |Serves 8

- 4 ounces bacon (about 4-5 slices), finely diced
- 10 large eggs
- 1/3 cup whole milk cottage cheese, drained
- 1 tablespoon Dijon mustard
- 1 medium red bell pepper, roasted, peeled and finely chopped
- Kosher salt and freshly ground black pepper, to taste
- ¼ cup fresh cilantro, finely chopped, plus extra for garnish
- Optional: paprika for garnish

1. Cook bacon in a medium skillet over medium heat until crispy, about 5-7 minutes. Transfer to a paper towel-lined plate using a slotted spoon. Reserve 1 tablespoon bacon fat if desired for mixing.
2. Place eggs in a large saucepan and cover with cold water by 1 inch. Bring to a rolling boil over high heat. Remove from heat, cover, and let stand for exactly 9 minutes for perfect hard-boiled eggs.
3. Prepare an ice bath while eggs cook. When timer ends, transfer eggs immediately to ice bath and let cool for 5 minutes.
4. Peel eggs under gently running cool water. Pat dry with paper towels. Cut eggs in half lengthwise.
5. Carefully remove yolks and place in a medium bowl. Arrange whites on a serving platter.
6. Using a fork, mash yolks until finely crumbled. Add cottage cheese, Dijon mustard, chopped roasted pepper, and half the bacon. Mix until smooth. Season with salt and pepper to taste.
7. Stir in 3 tablespoons of the chopped cilantro.
8. Transfer yolk mixture to a piping bag fitted with a large star tip (or use a zip-top bag with corner snipped) and pipe filling into egg white halves. Alternatively, spoon the mixture into the whites.
9. Garnish with remaining bacon, cilantro, and a light dusting of paprika if desired.

Per Serving

Calories: 293| Fat: 22.3g | Carbs: 4.8g | Protein: 18.6g | Fiber: 0.8g

CHAPTER 4:
LUNCHTIME BITES

TURKISH CHICKEN KEBABS

Prep time: 10 minutes | Cook time: 20 minutes |Serves 2

- 1 pound chicken thighs, boneless and skinless, halved
- ½ cup Greek-style yogurt
- Sea salt, to taste
- 1 tablespoon Aleppo red pepper flakes
- ½ teaspoon ground black pepper
- ¼ teaspoon dried oregano
- ½ teaspoon mustard seeds
- 1/8 teaspoon ground cinnamon
- ½ teaspoon sumac
- 2 Roma tomatoes, chopped
- 2 tablespoons olive oil
- 1 ½ ounces Swiss cheese, sliced

1. Place the chicken thighs, yogurt, salt, red pepper flakes, black pepper, oregano, mustard seeds, cinnamon, sumac, tomatoes, and olive oil in a ceramic dish. Cover and let it marinate in the refrigerator for 4 hours.
2. Preheat your grill to medium-high heat and lightly oil the grate. Thread the chicken thighs onto skewers, forming a thick log shape.
3. Cook the kebabs for 3–4 minutes per side, or until an instant-read thermometer reads 165°F.
4. Add the cheese and continue cooking for an additional 3–4 minutes, or until the cheese is fully melted. Serve immediately.

Per Serving

Calories: 498 | Fat: 23.2g | Carbs: 6.2g | Protein: 61g | Fiber: 1.7g

BEEF AND BROCCOLI

Prep time: 5 minutes | Cook time: 30 minutes | Serves 4

- 1 pound beef flank or skirt steak
- 1 tablespoon coconut oil
- ½ inch fresh ginger, peeled and minced
- 4 cups broccoli florets

Sauce

- ¼ cup coconut aminos
- 1 tablespoon arrowroot powder
- 2 teaspoons Thai fish sauce
- 1 teaspoon toasted sesame oil
- 5–10 drops liquid stevia (optional)

1. Slice the flank steak into thin slices.
2. Heat the coconut oil in a large pan over medium-high heat. Add the ginger and stir quickly.
3. Add the beef and cook for 8–10 minutes, until browned.
4. In a separate pot, bring 2–3 inches of water to a boil and steam the broccoli until fork-tender.
5. Stir together the sauce ingredients in a small bowl.
6. Add half of the broccoli to the pan with the beef, pour over the sauce, and stir until the sauce thickens.
7. Serve the beef mixture over the remaining broccoli.

Per Serving

Calories: 330 | Fat: 16.2g | Protein: 33.2g | Carbs: 11.4g | Fiber: 2.4g

CHICKEN SAUSAGE AND CABBAGE

Prep time: **5 minutes** | Cook time: **30 minutes** | Serves **2**

- 1 tablespoon avocado oil
- ½ yellow onion, sliced
- 2 garlic cloves, minced
- 2 links organic chicken sausage (no sugar added), sliced
- ¼ small green cabbage, shredded
- ¼ cup water
- Pinch of salt

1. Heat a large skillet over medium heat and add the avocado oil, onion, and garlic. Sauté for 4 to 5 minutes, or until the onion is translucent.
2. Add the chicken sausage and cook for 3 to 4 minutes on each side.
3. Add the cabbage, water, and salt. Cook for 5 minutes, or until the cabbage has softened and the water has evaporated. Serve warm.

Per Serving

Calories: **207** | Fat: **8g** | Protein: **17.7g** | Carbs: **16.1g** | Fiber: **4.2g**

EASY JERK RIBS

Prep time: **2 minutes** | Cook time: **1 hour 45 minutes** | Serves **4**

- 1 rack baby back ribs
- ¼ cup jerk seasoning
- 2 teaspoons kosher salt
- ½ cup Easy Keto BBQ Sauce

1. Preheat a grill to medium heat. Generously season the rack of ribs on both sides with the jerk seasoning and salt. Grill for 15 minutes per side over direct heat. The ribs should be browned and crispy-looking on the outside.
2. Wrap the ribs loosely in foil and place on the grill over indirect heat. You may need to move coals to the side or turn off one or two burners to create a flame-free space. With the lid closed, cook the ribs for 1 hour, maintaining a grill temperature of about 350°F.
3. After 1 hour, open the foil and baste the ribs on both sides with BBQ sauce. Cook for 30 more minutes, or until the ribs are done to your desired tenderness. Cut into individual ribs to serve.

Per Serving

Calories: **390** | Fat: **27g** | Protein: **26g** | Carbs: **6g** | Fiber: **2g**

SHREDDED BEEF WITH HERBS

Prep time: 5 minutes | Cook time: 50 minutes | Serves 4

- 1 tablespoon olive oil
- 1 pound ribeye steak, cut into strips
- 2 tablespoons rice wine
- ¼ cup beef bone broth
- Sea salt and freshly ground black pepper, to taste
- 2 tablespoons fresh parsley, finely chopped
- 2 tablespoons fresh chives, finely chopped
- 2 chipotle peppers in adobo sauce, chopped
- 1 garlic clove, crushed
- 2 small tomatoes, pureed
- 1 yellow onion, peeled and chopped
- ½ teaspoon dry mustard
- 1 teaspoon dried basil
- 1 teaspoon dried marjoram

1. Heat oil in a pan over medium-high heat. Sear the beef strips for 6–7 minutes, stirring occasionally. Work in batches if necessary.
2. Add the remaining ingredients, reduce the heat to medium-low, and cook for 40 minutes.
3. Shred the beef and serve.

Per Serving

Calories: **421** | Fat: **35.7g** | Carbs: **5.9g** | Fiber: **1g** | Protein: **19.7g**

BUFFALO CHICKEN WINGS

Prep time: 5 minutes | Cook time: 1 hour, 10 minutes | Serves 2

- 6 whole chicken wings
- 1 tablespoon avocado oil
- 1 teaspoon sea salt
- 4 tablespoons grass-fed butter or ghee
- ¼ cup hot sauce of your choice
- 1 garlic clove, minced, or 1 teaspoon garlic powder

1. Preheat the oven to 400°F.
2. In a bowl, toss the chicken wings in the avocado oil and sea salt. Set a wire rack on a baking sheet and arrange the chicken wings with space left between them.
3. Bake for 20 minutes. Increase the oven temperature to 425°F and bake for an additional 10 minutes. Ensure the chicken is cooked through and the internal temperature reaches 165°F.
4. In a small saucepan over medium-low heat, place the butter or ghee, hot sauce, and minced garlic and heat, stirring frequently, until the butter has melted.
5. Toss the chicken wings in the warm sauce and serve immediately.

Per Serving

Calories: **351** | Fat: **29.5g** | Protein: **19.4g** | Carbs: **0.9g** | Fiber: **0.3g**

PORK AND SAUSAGE ENDIVE WRAPS

Prep time: **5 minutes** | Cook time: **15 minutes** |Serves **6**

- 2 tablespoons olive oil
- 1 ½ pounds ground pork
- 2 ounces pork sausage, crumbled
- ½ cup yellow onion, chopped
- 2 bell peppers, chopped
- 1 jalapeño pepper, chopped
- 2 cloves garlic, finely chopped
- ¼ teaspoon ground bay leaf
- Sea salt and freshly ground black pepper, to taste
- 18 endive spears, rinsed

1. Heat olive oil in a large saucepan over medium-high heat. Cook the ground pork and sausage until browned, about 3 minutes.
2. Add the onion and bell peppers. Stir until the vegetables soften, then add the jalapeño, garlic, bay leaf, salt, and pepper. Continue stirring for another 30 seconds.
3. Spoon the meat mixture onto the endive spears and serve.

Per Serving

Calories:433 | 30.1g Fat:| Carbs: 6g | Protein: 33.2g | Fiber: 3.2g

TUNA, AVOCADO AND HAM WRAPS

Prep time: **5 minutes** | Cook time: **10 minutes** |Serves **3**

- ½ cup dry white wine
- ½ cup water
- ½ teaspoon mixed peppercorns
- ½ teaspoon dry mustard powder
- ½ pound ahi tuna steak
- 6 slices of ham
- ½ Hass avocado, peeled, pitted, and sliced
- 1 tablespoon fresh lemon juice
- 6 lettuce leaves

1. Add wine, water, peppercorns, and mustard powder to a skillet and bring to a boil. Add the tuna and simmer gently for 3 to 5 minutes per side.
2. Discard the cooking liquid and slice the tuna into bite-sized pieces. Divide the tuna pieces between slices of ham.
3. Add avocado and drizzle with fresh lemon. Roll the wraps up and place each wrap on a lettuce leaf. Serve well chilled. Bon appétit!

Per Serving

Calories: 408 | Fat: 19.9g | Carbs: 4.3g | Fiber: 2.5g | Protein: 27.8g

GREEN CHICKEN CURRY

Prep time: **5 minutes** | Cook time: **12 minutes** | Serves **4**

- 3 tablespoons green curry paste
- 1 tablespoon coconut oil
- 1 (14-ounce) can full-fat unsweetened coconut milk
- 3 tablespoons granulated erythritol
- 2 tablespoons fish sauce (no sugar added)
- 2 cups broccoli florets
- 1 pound boneless, skinless chicken breasts, cut into thin strips
- ½ cup sliced yellow bell peppers
- ½ cup sliced bamboo shoots, drained
- 1 tablespoon sliced chili peppers
- Fresh cilantro leaves, for garnish

1. Combine the curry paste and coconut oil in a large skillet and cook over medium heat for 2 minutes, or until fragrant.
2. Whisk in the coconut milk, sweetener, and fish sauce until smooth. Add the broccoli and simmer over medium-low heat for 5 minutes, being careful not to allow the mixture to boil.
3. Add the chicken, bell peppers, bamboo shoots, and chili peppers. Simmer, stirring occasionally, for another 5 minutes, or until the chicken is cooked through and the broccoli is fork-tender. Garnish with cilantro and serve hot.

Per Serving

Calories: **391** | Fat: **20g** | Protein: **29g** | Carbs: **8g** | Fiber: **4g**

SEA BASS WITH DIJON BUTTER SAUCE

Prep time: **5 minutes** | Cook time: **20 minutes** | Serves **3**

- 2 tablespoons olive oil
- 2 sea bass fillets
- ¼ teaspoon red pepper flakes, crushed
- Sea salt, to taste
- 1/3 teaspoon mixed peppercorns, crushed
- 3 tablespoons butter
- 1 tablespoon Dijon mustard
- 2 cloves garlic, minced
- 1 tablespoon fresh lime juice

1. Heat the olive oil in a skillet over medium-high heat.
2. Pat dry the sea bass fillets with paper towels. Pan-fry the fish fillets for about 4 minutes on each side until the flesh flakes easily and the fish is nearly opaque.
3. Season the fish with red pepper flakes, sea salt, and mixed peppercorns.
4. To make the sauce, melt the butter in a saucepan over low heat; stir in the Dijon mustard, garlic, and lime juice. Let it simmer for 2 minutes.
5. Spoon the Dijon butter sauce over the fish fillets. Bon appétit!

Per Serving

Calories: **314** | Fat: **23.2g** | Carbs: **1.4g** | Protein: **24.2g** | Fiber: **0.3g**

FISH TACO BOWL

Prep time: 10 minutes | Cook time: 15 minutes | Serves 2

- 2 (5-ounce) tilapia fillets
- 1 tablespoon olive oil
- 4 teaspoons Tajín seasoning salt, divided
- 2 cups pre-sliced coleslaw cabbage mix
- 1 tablespoon Spicy Red Pepper Miso Mayo, plus more for serving
- 1 avocado, mashed
- Pink Himalayan salt, to taste
- Freshly ground black pepper, to taste

1. Preheat the oven to 425°F. Line a baking sheet with aluminum foil or a silicone baking mat.
2. Rub the tilapia with olive oil, then coat it with 2 teaspoons of Tajín seasoning salt. Place the fish in the prepared pan.
3. Bake for 15 minutes, or until the fish is opaque when pierced with a fork. Let the fish sit on a cooling rack for 4 minutes.
4. Meanwhile, in a medium bowl, gently mix the coleslaw and mayo sauce. You don't want the cabbage to be too wet—just enough to dress it. Add the mashed avocado and remaining 2 teaspoons of Tajín seasoning salt to the coleslaw. Season with pink Himalayan salt and freshly ground black pepper.
5. Divide the salad between two bowls. Use two forks to shred the fish into small pieces and add to the bowls.
6. Top the fish with a drizzle of mayo sauce and serve.

Per Serving

Calories: **315** | Fat: **24g** | Carbs: **12g** | Fiber: **7g** | Protein: **16g**

BUTTERY HERB CHICKEN

Prep time: 5 minutes | Cook time: 20 minutes |Serves 4

- 2 tablespoons butter, softened at room temperature
- 5 skinless chicken legs
- 2 scallions, chopped
- 1 teaspoon fresh basil, chopped
- 1 teaspoon fresh thyme, chopped
- 1 garlic clove, minced
- ½ teaspoon freshly cracked black pepper
- 1 cup vegetable broth
- ½ teaspoon paprika
- Sea salt, to taste

1. Melt 1 tablespoon of butter in a frying pan over medium-high heat. Brown the chicken legs for 4–5 minutes per side.
2. Add the scallions, basil, thyme, and garlic. Sauté for about a minute.
3. Add the remaining tablespoon of butter, black pepper, broth, and paprika. Bring to a boil, then reduce the heat to a simmer.
4. Let it simmer for 10 minutes or until fully cooked. Season with salt to taste and serve.

Per Serving

Calories: **370** | Fat: **16g** | Carbs: **0.9g** | Protein: **51g** | Fiber: **0.2g**

CHAPTER 5: DINNER DELIGHTS

MARINATED SKIRT STEAK

Prep time: 10 minutes | Cook time: 6-8 minutes | Serves 6

- 2 pounds skirt steak, trimmed
- ¼ cup sugar-free balsamic vinegar
- 2 tablespoons extra-virgin olive oil
- 2 tablespoons fresh parsley, finely chopped
- 3 cloves garlic, minced
- 1 teaspoon kosher salt
- ½ teaspoon freshly ground black pepper

1. Whisk together all marinade ingredients in a large bowl.
2. Place steak in a large resealable plastic bag or shallow dish and pour marinade over it. Turn to coat evenly.
3. Refrigerate for at least 2 hours or up to 24 hours, turning occasionally.
4. Remove steak from refrigerator 30 minutes before cooking to reach room temperature.
5. Preheat grill to high heat (450-500°F).
6. Remove steak from marinade, reserving liquid. Pat steak dry with paper towels.
7. Grill 3-4 minutes per side for medium-rare (135°F internal temperature) or 4-5 minutes for medium (140°F).
8. Meanwhile, pour reserved marinade into a small saucepan. Bring to a full boil over high heat and cook for 3 minutes to create a sauce.
9. Let steak rest for 10 minutes before slicing against the grain at a 45-degree angle.
10. Serve with the reduced marinade sauce.

Per Serving

Calories: 354 | Fat: 25g | Protein: 31g | Carbs:0g | Fiber:0g | Net Carbs:0g

KETO STREET TACOS

Prep time: 15 minutes | Cook time: 20 minutes |Serves 4

- ½ pound ground pork
- ½ pound ground turkey
- 1 teaspoon kosher salt
- ½ teaspoon fresh ground black pepper
- 2 tablespoons avocado oil or lard
- ½ cup sugar-free roasted tomatillo salsa
- 12 large butter lettuce leaves
- ½ cup fresh cilantro, chopped
- ½ cup sour cream
- 1 lime, cut into wedges

1. In a large bowl, combine ground pork, turkey, salt, and pepper until well mixed.
2. Heat oil in a large skillet over medium-high heat.
3. Add meat mixture and cook for 7-8 minutes, breaking up with a spatula until well-browned.
4. Stir in tomatillo salsa and cook 2-3 minutes more until heated through.
5. Arrange lettuce leaves on a serving platter.
6. Divide meat mixture among lettuce leaves.
7. Top each taco with cilantro and a dollop of sour cream.
8. Serve immediately with lime wedges.

Per Serving

Calories: 330 | Fat: 26.3g | Carbs: 4.9g | Fiber: 1.3g | Protein: 17.9g

PAN-SEARED SALMON WITH BRAISED KALE

Prep time: 15 minutes | Cook time:15 minutes |Serves 4

- 4 (6-ounce) salmon fillets
- ¾ cup sugar-free vinaigrette
- 1 medium red onion, thinly sliced
- 4 cups fresh kale, stems removed and roughly chopped
- ¼ teaspoon red pepper flakes
- ½ teaspoon sea salt
- 2 tablespoons olive oil

1. Place salmon in a shallow dish and pour ½ cup vinaigrette over top. Marinate in refrigerator for 30 minutes to 2 hours.
2. Heat olive oil in a large skillet over medium-high heat.
3. Remove salmon from marinade (discard used marinade) and pat dry with paper towels.
4. Place salmon skin-side up in the hot pan. Cook for 4 minutes until golden brown.
5. Flip salmon and add onions around the fillets. Cook 3-4 minutes more.
6. Add kale, remaining vinaigrette, red pepper flakes, and salt to the pan.
7. Cover and cook 2-3 minutes until kale is wilted and salmon is cooked through (internal temperature 145°F).

Per Serving

Calories: 438 | Fat: 33 g | Carbs: 9.1 g | Fiber: 3.3 g | Protein: 26.3 g

CAULIFLOWER LOBSTER RISOTTO

Prep time: 20 minutes | Cook time: 25 minutes | Serves 3

- 3 (4-ounce) lobster tails
- 3 cups salted water
- 2 tablespoons butter
- 3 cups cauliflower rice (about 1 medium head)
- ½ teaspoon kosher salt
- ¼ teaspoon white pepper
- ⅓ cup dry sherry
- 4 ounces mascarpone cheese
- ¼ cup freshly grated Parmesan cheese
- 2 tablespoons chopped scallions, plus more for garnish

1. Bring salted water to boil in a medium saucepan.
2. Add lobster tails and cook for 5-6 minutes until shells turn bright red.
3. Remove lobster, reserving ¼ cup cooking liquid. Let lobster cool slightly.
4. Remove meat from shells. Set aside two half-tails for garnish, chop remaining meat.
5. Heat butter in a large skillet over medium heat.
6. Add cauliflower rice, salt, and pepper. Cook 5 minutes, stirring occasionally.
7. Add sherry and reserved cooking liquid. Cook 4-5 minutes until liquid is mostly absorbed.
8. Fold in mascarpone, Parmesan, scallions, and chopped lobster.
9. Cook 2-3 minutes until heated through and creamy.
10. Serve topped with reserved lobster tail meat and additional scallions.

Per Serving

Calories: 449 | Fat: 30g | Protein: 41g | Carbs: 8g | Fiber: 3g

TEXAS-STYLE KETO CHILI

Prep time: 15 minutes | **Cook time: 45 minutes** | Serves **6**

- 2 tablespoons tallow or avocado oil
- 1 large bell pepper, diced
- 1 medium leek, white and light green parts only, cleaned and chopped
- 2 celery ribs, diced
- 2 pounds ground beef
- 3 cloves garlic, minced
- 2 large tomatoes, pureed (about 2 cups)
- 2 cups low-sodium chicken broth
- 1 tablespoon Mexican oregano
- 1-2 teaspoons chipotle powder (adjust to taste)
- 1½ teaspoons kosher salt
- 1 teaspoon black pepper
- Sour cream (Optional)

1. Heat tallow in a large Dutch oven over medium-high heat.
2. Add bell pepper, leek, and celery. Cook 3-4 minutes until softened.
3. Add ground beef, breaking up with a wooden spoon. Cook until browned, about 5-7 minutes.
4. Add garlic and cook 1 minute until fragrant.
5. Stir in pureed tomatoes, broth, oregano, chipotle powder, salt, and pepper.
6. Bring to a boil, reduce heat to low, and simmer uncovered for 30-35 minutes until thickened.
7. Adjust seasonings to taste.
8. Serve hot with optional toppings.

Per Serving

Calories: 412 | **Fat: 28g** | **Protein: 35g** | **Carbs: 6g** | **Fiber: 1.5g**

CREAMY CHICKEN ALFREDO

Prep time: 15 minutes | **Cook time: 25 minutes** | Serves **4**

- 4 boneless, skinless chicken breasts (about 6 ounces each)
- 2 tablespoons olive oil
- 2 cloves garlic, minced
- 1 cup heavy cream
- 1 cup freshly grated Parmesan cheese
- ½ teaspoon Italian seasoning
- 1 teaspoon kosher salt
- ½ teaspoon black pepper
- 2 tablespoons fresh parsley, chopped

1. Pat chicken breasts dry. If thick, butterfly or pound to even ¾-inch thickness.
2. Season chicken with ½ teaspoon salt and ¼ teaspoon pepper.
3. Heat olive oil in a large skillet over medium-high heat.
4. Cook chicken 6-7 minutes per side until golden and internal temperature reaches 165°F.
5. Transfer chicken to a plate and tent with foil.
6. Reduce heat to medium-low. Add garlic to same skillet and cook 1 minute.
7. Add cream and bring to gentle simmer. Cook 2-3 minutes until slightly reduced.
8. Stir in Parmesan, Italian seasoning, remaining salt and pepper.
9. Simmer 3-4 minutes until sauce thickens enough to coat back of spoon.
10. Slice chicken against grain and return to pan; coat with sauce.
11. Garnish with fresh parsley before serving.

Per Serving

Calories: 470 | **Fat: 35g** | **Carbs: 6g** | **Fiber: 1g** | **Protein: 38g**

ZUCCHINI LASAGNA

Prep time: 30 minutes | Cook time: 50 minutes | Serves 6

- 4 medium zucchini (about 2 pounds)
- 1 pound ground beef (80/20)
- 1 tablespoon olive oil
- ½ medium onion, finely diced
- 3 cloves garlic, minced
- 1 cup sugar-free marinara sauce
- 1½ cups whole milk ricotta cheese
- 1½ cups shredded mozzarella cheese, divided
- ½ cup freshly grated Parmesan cheese
- 1 large egg
- 1 teaspoon Italian seasoning
- 1 teaspoon kosher salt
- ½ teaspoon black pepper
- Fresh basil leaves for garnish

1. Preheat oven to 375°F.
2. Trim ends off zucchini. Using a mandoline or sharp knife, slice lengthwise into ⅛-inch thick strips.
3. Arrange zucchini on paper towel-lined baking sheets. Sprinkle with salt and let drain 15 minutes.
4. Meanwhile, heat oil in large skillet over medium-high heat.
5. Add ground beef and onion. Cook 6-8 minutes, breaking up meat, until beef is browned.
6. Add garlic and cook 1 minute more.
7. Stir in marinara sauce and simmer 5 minutes. Season with ½ teaspoon salt and ¼ teaspoon pepper.
8. In medium bowl, combine ricotta, 1 cup mozzarella, Parmesan, egg, Italian seasoning, and remaining salt and pepper.
9. Pat zucchini dry with paper towels.
10. Layer in 9x13 baking dish:
    - Layer of zucchini strips
    - Half of meat sauce
    - Half of cheese mixture
    - Repeat layers
    - Top with remaining ½ cup mozzarella
11. Cover with foil and bake 30 minutes.
12. Uncover and bake 15-20 minutes until bubbly and cheese is golden.
13. Let rest 10 minutes before serving. Garnish with fresh basil.

Per Serving

Calories: **380** | Fat: **27g** | Carbs: **7g** | Fiber: **2g** | Protein: **31g**

ASIAN-STYLE SHRIMP AND BROCCOLI

Prep time: 10 minutes | **Cook time: 15 minutes** | Serves **4**

- 1 pound large shrimp (21-25 count), peeled and deveined
- 3 cups broccoli florets
- 1 medium red bell pepper, sliced
- 2 tablespoons coconut oil
- 3 cloves garlic, minced
- 2 tablespoons coconut aminos (or tamari for gluten-free)
- 1 tablespoon toasted sesame oil
- 1 tablespoon rice vinegar
- ½ teaspoon red pepper flakes (optional)
- 1 teaspoon kosher salt
- ½ teaspoon black pepper
- 2 tablespoons toasted sesame seeds

1. Pat shrimp dry with paper towels. Season with ½ teaspoon salt and ¼ teaspoon pepper.
2. Heat 1 tablespoon coconut oil in large wok or skillet over high heat.
3. Add shrimp in single layer. Cook 2 minutes per side until pink and just cooked through.
4. Transfer shrimp to plate.
5. Add remaining coconut oil to pan.
6. Add broccoli and bell pepper. Stir-fry 4-5 minutes until crisp-tender.
7. Add garlic, cook 30 seconds until fragrant.
8. Add coconut aminos, sesame oil, vinegar, pepper flakes, remaining salt and pepper.
9. Return shrimp to pan; toss until heated through.
10. Garnish with sesame seeds and serve hot.

Per Serving

Calories: 320 | **Fat: 22g** | **Carbs: 7g** | **Fiber: 3g** | **Protein: 29g**

CHAPTER 6: SALADS AND SOUPS

CLASSIC EGG SALAD

Prep time: 5 minutes | **Cook time:15 minutes** |**Serves 2**

- 6 large eggs
- ¼ cup scallions, finely chopped
- 1 jalapeño pepper, seeded and minced
- ½ cup mayonnaise
- 1 tablespoon Dijon mustard
- ½ teaspoon kosher salt
- ¼ teaspoon black pepper
- 2 tablespoons fresh parsley, chopped
- ½ teaspoon sweet paprika

1. Place eggs in a medium saucepan and cover with cold water by 1 inch.
2. Bring to rolling boil over high heat.
3. Remove from heat, cover, and let stand 10 minutes.
4. Transfer eggs to bowl of ice water; let cool 5 minutes.
5. Peel eggs under cool running water.
6. Chop eggs into ½-inch pieces.
7. In large bowl, combine eggs, scallions, jalapeño, mayonnaise, and mustard.
8. Season with salt and pepper; mix gently.
9. Garnish with parsley and paprika.
10. Chill at least 30 minutes before serving.

Per Serving

Calories: 398 | Fat: 35.2g | Carbs: 5.5g | Protein: 14.6g | Fiber: 1g

SHRIMP CAPRESE SALAD

Prep time: 15 minutes | **Chill time: 30 minutes** | **Serves 4**

- 1 pound large shrimp (21-25 count), peeled, deveined, and cooked
- 1 cup cherry tomatoes, halved
- 4 ounces fresh mozzarella pearls (or cubed if using larger size)
- ¼ cup fresh basil leaves, thinly sliced
- ¼ cup prepared Creamy Basil-Parmesan Vinaigrette
- ¼ teaspoon kosher salt
- ¼ teaspoon black pepper
- Extra basil leaves for garnish

1. Halve the cooked shrimp lengthwise.
2. In a large bowl, combine shrimp, tomatoes, mozzarella, and sliced basil.
3. Add vinaigrette, salt, and pepper. Toss gently to combine.
4. Cover and refrigerate 30 minutes to allow flavors to meld.
5. Before serving, toss again and adjust seasoning if needed.
6. Garnish with additional basil leaves.

Per Serving

Calories: 371 | Fat: 27g | Protein: 30g | Carbs: 3g | Fiber: 1g

SALMON LETTUCE CUPS

Prep time: 10 minutes | Cook time: 5 minutes |Serves 4

- 2 (6-ounce) cans wild-caught salmon, drained
- ½ cup mayonnaise
- 3 tablespoons prepared horseradish
- 2 tablespoons fresh dill, chopped
- 2 teaspoons fresh lemon juice
- ½ teaspoon sea salt
- ½ teaspoon black pepper

For Serving:

- 12 butter lettuce leaves, cleaned and dried
- Extra dill sprigs for garnish
- Lemon wedges

1. Drain salmon well, remove any bones if desired.
2. In medium bowl, combine salmon, mayonnaise, horseradish, dill, lemon juice, salt, and pepper.
3. Mix gently, breaking salmon into small flakes.
4. Arrange lettuce leaves on serving platter.
5. Divide salmon mixture among lettuce cups (about 3 tablespoons each).
6. Garnish with dill sprigs and serve with lemon wedges.

Per Serving

Calories: **314** | Fat: **26.5 g** | Carbs: **4.4 g** | Fiber: **1.1 g** | Protein: **14.6 g**

CLASSIC COBB SALAD

Prep time: 10 minutes | Cook time: 5 minutes | Serves 4

- 4 cups mixed salad greens (romaine, baby spinach, and arugula blend)
- 1 cup diced cooked chicken breast
- 4 large hard-boiled eggs, quartered
- 1 medium ripe avocado, diced
- ½ cup crumbled blue cheese
- 6 slices crispy bacon, crumbled
- 1 cup cherry tomatoes, halved
- ¼ cup extra-virgin olive oil
- 2 tablespoons red wine vinegar
- ½ teaspoon kosher salt
- ¼ teaspoon freshly ground black pepper

1. In a large serving bowl, arrange the salad greens as the base layer.
2. Arrange rows of diced chicken, egg quarters, diced avocado, blue cheese crumbles, bacon pieces, and halved tomatoes across the greens.
3. In a small bowl, whisk together the olive oil, red wine vinegar, salt, and pepper until well combined.
4. Just before serving, drizzle the dressing over the salad and toss gently to combine.

Per Serving

Calories: **420** | Fat: **33g** | Carbs: **7g** | Fiber: **5g** | Protein: **30g**

CHILLED SHRIMP AND AVOCADO SALAD

Prep time: **15 minutes** | Cook time: **30 minutes** | Serves 3

- 1 pound medium shrimp, peeled and deveined
- 1 tablespoon olive oil
- ½ teaspoon kosher salt
- ¼ teaspoon black pepper
- 1 large ripe avocado, cubed
- 1 celery stalk, finely diced
- ⅓ cup mayonnaise
- 1 tablespoon fresh lime juice
- 1 tablespoon fresh cilantro, chopped (optional)
- Lettuce leaves for serving (optional)

1. If using raw shrimp: Heat olive oil in large skillet over medium-high heat.
2. Season shrimp with ¼ teaspoon each salt and pepper.
3. Cook shrimp 2 minutes per side until pink and opaque.
4. Transfer to bowl and refrigerate until chilled, about 15 minutes.
5. Meanwhile, in medium bowl, combine avocado, celery, mayonnaise, lime juice, and remaining salt.
6. When shrimp are chilled, cut into ½-inch pieces if large.
7. Fold shrimp into avocado mixture.
8. Adjust seasoning to taste.
9. Cover and chill 30 minutes.
10. Serve on lettuce leaves if desired, garnished with cilantro.

Per Serving

Calories: **571** | Fat: **41g** | Carbs: **8g** | Fiber: **5g** | Protein: **50g**

CREAMY CAULIFLOWER SOUP

Prep time: **10 minutes** | Cook time: **25 minutes** | Serves 6

- 2 tablespoons olive oil
- 1 medium yellow onion, diced
- 3 cloves garlic, minced
- 2 pounds cauliflower florets (about 1 large head)
- 4 cups low-sodium chicken broth
- 1 cup heavy whipping cream
- 1 teaspoon dried thyme
- 1 teaspoon kosher salt
- ½ teaspoon freshly ground black pepper
- ½ cup freshly grated Parmesan cheese
- 2 tablespoons fresh parsley, chopped, for garnish

1. Heat olive oil in a large Dutch oven over medium heat. Add onion and garlic, sautéing until softened and translucent, about 3-4 minutes.
2. Add cauliflower florets and chicken broth. Bring to a boil, then reduce heat to low and simmer, covered, for 15-20 minutes until cauliflower is fork-tender.
3. Using an immersion blender, puree the soup until completely smooth. (Alternatively, carefully transfer to a blender in batches.)
4. Stir in heavy cream, thyme, salt, pepper, and Parmesan cheese. Simmer for an additional 5 minutes.
5. Taste and adjust seasoning if needed. Serve hot, garnished with fresh parsley.

Per Serving

Calories: **220** | Fat: **18g** | Carbs: **7g** | Fiber: **3g** | Protein: **6g**

GRILLED CHICKEN CAESAR SALAD

Prep time: **10 minutes** | Cook time: **10 minutes** | Serves **4**

- 2 pounds boneless, skinless chicken breasts
- 2 tablespoons olive oil
- 8 cups hearts of romaine, roughly chopped
- ½ cup freshly grated Parmesan cheese
- ½ cup keto-friendly Caesar dressing
- 1 teaspoon kosher salt
- ½ teaspoon freshly ground black pepper
- ¼ cup fresh parsley, chopped

1. Brush chicken breasts with 1 tablespoon olive oil and season with ½ teaspoon each salt and pepper.
2. Heat a large skillet or grill pan over medium-high heat. Cook chicken for 5-6 minutes per side until internal temperature reaches 165°F. Let rest for 5 minutes, then slice against the grain.
3. In a large bowl, toss romaine lettuce with remaining olive oil and Caesar dressing until evenly coated.
4. Divide dressed lettuce among four plates. Top with sliced chicken, Parmesan cheese, and parsley.
5. Season with additional salt and pepper if desired. Serve immediately.

Per Serving

Calories: **400** | Fat: **28g** | Carbs: **4g** | Fiber: **2g** | Protein: **35g**

SPINACH AND MUSHROOM SOUP

Prep time: **10 minutes** | Cook time: **20 minutes** | Serves **4**

- 2 tablespoons unsalted butter
- 1 medium yellow onion, diced
- 3 cloves garlic, minced
- 16 ounces cremini mushrooms, sliced
- 6 cups fresh baby spinach, packed
- 4 cups low-sodium chicken broth
- 1 cup heavy whipping cream
- 1 teaspoon dried thyme
- 1 teaspoon kosher salt
- ½ teaspoon freshly ground black pepper
- ½ cup freshly grated Parmesan cheese

1. In a large Dutch oven, melt butter over medium heat. Add onion and garlic, cooking until softened, about 3-4 minutes.
2. Add mushrooms and cook until they release their moisture and begin to brown, 5-7 minutes.
3. Add spinach and cook until wilted, about 2 minutes.
4. Pour in chicken broth, heavy cream, thyme, salt, and pepper. Bring to a gentle boil, then reduce heat and simmer for 10 minutes.
5. Using an immersion blender, puree until smooth. (Alternatively, carefully transfer to a blender in batches.)
6. Stir in Parmesan cheese until melted. Taste and adjust seasoning as needed.
7. Serve hot, garnished with additional Parmesan if desired.

Per Serving

Calories: **325** | Fat: **28g** | Carbs: **6g** | Fiber: **3g** | Protein: **6g**

CHAPTER 7: VEGETABLES & SIDE DISHES

SPANISH-STYLE STUFFED PEPPERS

Prep time: **5 minutes** | Cook time: **25 minutes** |Serves **4**

- 1 tablespoon olive oil
- 1 Spanish onion, chopped
- 1 teaspoon garlic, minced
- 1 cup vegetable broth
- 8 ounces chorizo sausage, chopped into small chunks
- 1 ripe tomato, chopped
- 6 ounces ricotta cheese
- Sea salt and ground black pepper, to taste
- 4 red bell peppers, halved and seeds removed
- 2 ounces Swiss cheese, shredded

1. Heat olive oil in a sauté pan over medium heat. Sauté the onion and garlic for 2 minutes, or until tender and fragrant.
2. Add a splash of vegetable broth to deglaze the pan. Add chorizo, tomato, and ricotta cheese. Season with salt and black pepper.
3. Microwave the red peppers for about 8 minutes, or until they soften.
4. Stuff the pepper halves with the chorizo mixture and place them in a lightly oiled baking dish. Pour the remaining broth around the stuffed peppers.
5. Bake in the preheated oven at 420°F for 9 minutes. Top with Swiss cheese and bake for an additional 4 to 5 minutes. Enjoy!

Per Serving

Calories: **340** | Fat: **27.2g** | Carbs: **5.2g** | Protein: **14.7g** | Fiber: **1.5g**

STUFFED SPAGHETTI SQUASH BOWLS

Prep time: **5 minutes** | Cook time: **1 hour** |Serves **4**

- ½ pound spaghetti squash, halved, seeds scooped out
- 2 teaspoons olive oil
- ½ cup shredded mozzarella cheese
- ½ cup cream cheese
- ½ cup full-fat Greek yogurt
- 2 large eggs
- 1 garlic clove, minced
- ½ teaspoon cumin
- ½ teaspoon basil
- ½ teaspoon mint
- **Sea salt and black pepper, to taste**

1. Place the squash halves in a baking pan and drizzle the insides with olive oil.
2. Bake in the preheated oven at 370°F for 45 to 50 minutes, or until the interiors are easily pierced with a fork.
3. Scrape the spaghetti squash "noodles" from the skin into a mixing bowl. Add the remaining ingredients and mix to combine.
4. Carefully fill each squash half with the cheese mixture. Bake at 350°F for 5 to 10 minutes, or until the cheese is bubbly and golden brown. Enjoy!

Per Serving

Calories: **219** | Fat: **17.5g** | Carbs: **6.9g** | Fiber: **0.9g** | Protein: **9g**

CAULIFLOWER RICE

Prep time: **15 minutes** | Cook time: **15 minutes** | Serves **4**

- ⅓ cup lard
- 4 cups riced cauliflower florets
- 1 cup chicken bone broth
- ½ teaspoon finely ground gray sea salt

1. Place the lard in a large frying pan over medium heat. When melted, add the remaining ingredients. Cover and cook for 8 to 10 minutes, until the cauliflower rice is tender.
2. Remove the lid and cook for another 5 minutes, or until the liquid has evaporated.
3. Divide the rice among 4 small bowls and serve.

Per Serving

Calories: **200** | Fat: **17.2g** | Carbs: **6.6g** | Fiber: **3.1g** | Protein: **4.6g**

BROCCOLI SLAW WITH TAHINI DRESSING

Prep time: **5 minutes** | Cook time: **10 minutes** | Serves **2**

- ½ cup broccoli florets
- 1 bell pepper, seeded and sliced
- 1 shallot, thinly sliced
- ½ cup arugula
- 2 ounces mozzarella cheese
- 2 tablespoons toasted sunflower seeds
- 1 tablespoon freshly squeezed lemon juice
- ¼ cup tahini (sesame butter)
- 1 garlic clove, minced
- ½ teaspoon yellow mustard
- ½ teaspoon black pepper
- Pink salt, to taste

1. Place the cabbage, pepper, shallot, and arugula in a salad bowl.
2. In a separate bowl, mix together all ingredients for the dressing.
3. Dress the salad and top with mozzarella cheese and sunflower seeds.
4. Serve at room temperature or well chilled. Enjoy!

Per Serving

Calories: **323** | Fat: **25.3g** | Carbs: **6.8g** | Protein: **15.7g** | Fiber: **3.4g**

CLASSIC CREAMED SWISS CHARD

Prep time: **5 minutes** | Cook time:**15 minutes** |Serves 6

- 2 tablespoons butter
- 1 yellow onion, chopped
- 2 garlic cloves, minced
- ½ teaspoon kosher salt
- ¼ teaspoon ground black pepper
- ¼ teaspoon dried oregano
- ¼ teaspoon dried dill
- 1 ½ pounds Swiss chard
- ½ cup vegetable broth
- 2 tablespoons dry white wine
- 1 cup sour cream

1. Melt the butter in a saucepan over medium heat. Sauté the onion for about 4 minutes, or until tender and fragrant.
2. Stir in the garlic and cook for 1 minute, or until aromatic. Add the salt, black pepper, oregano, and dill.
3. Add the Swiss chard in batches, folding it in. Pour in the vegetable broth and cook for 5 minutes, or until the chard wilts.
4. Stir in the wine and sour cream, and cook for an additional minute until everything is well combined. Serve hot.

Per Serving

Calories: **149** | Fat: **11.1g** | Carbs: **6.6g** | Protein: **5.4g** | Fiber: **2.2g**

BAKED ZUCCHINI FRIES

Prep time: **5 minutes** | Cook time: **40 minutes** | Serves 2

- 1 large or 2 small zucchinis
- ¼ cup almond flour
- 1 teaspoon paprika
- ½ teaspoon sea salt
- 1 large egg

1. Preheat the oven to 375°F. Line a baking sheet with parchment paper.
2. Slice the zucchini into "fries" and set them on a paper towel to drain for 5 minutes.
3. In a small bowl, mix together the almond flour, paprika, and salt. In another bowl, whisk the egg.
4. Dip each zucchini piece first in the egg, then in the almond flour mixture. Place the fries on the prepared baking sheet.
5. Bake for 15 minutes. Carefully flip them and bake for another 10 minutes, or until golden brown.
6. Serve warm.

Per Serving

Calories: **80** | Fat: **4.4g** | Protein: **5.6g** | Carbs: **6.9g** | Fiber: **2.6g**

CHEESY BROCCOLI

Prep time: 5 minutes | **Cook time: 30 minutes** | **Serves 4**

- 1 pound broccoli florets (fresh or frozen)
- 4 tablespoons grass-fed butter, ghee, or coconut oil
- ½ teaspoon sea salt
- 1 cup shredded cheddar cheese
- ¼ cup freshly grated Parmesan cheese

1. Preheat the oven to 400°F.
2. Bring 1 inch of water to a boil in a large pot over medium-high heat. Add the broccoli, cover, and cook for 5 minutes.
3. Drain the broccoli and place it in a greased medium casserole dish.
4. Add the butter and mix well. Top with salt and cheese.
5. Bake for 20 minutes, or until the cheese begins to brown.

Per Serving

Calories: 297 | **Fat: 25.1g** | **Protein: 12.9g** | **Carbs: 8.2g** | **Fiber: 3g**

HERBED RADISHES

Prep time: 10 minutes | **Cook time: 15 minutes** | **Serves 2**

- 3 tablespoons lard
- 14 ounces radishes (about 2 bunches), quartered
- ⅛ teaspoon sea salt
- ⅛ teaspoon black pepper
- 2 tablespoons sliced fresh chives
- 1 tablespoon chopped fresh herbs, such as thyme and/or rosemary

1. Heat the lard in a large frying pan over medium heat until melted. Add the quartered radishes, salt, and pepper. Cover and cook for 5 minutes, or until softened.
2. Remove the lid and cook for another 7 minutes, stirring frequently, until the radishes begin to brown.
3. Add the chives and fresh herbs, tossing to combine. Reduce the heat to medium-low and continue to cook for 2 minutes.
4. Remove from the heat, divide among 4 small bowls, and serve.

Per Serving

Calories: 223 | **Fat: 19.3g** | **Carbs: 6.6g** | **Fiber: 0.6g** | **Protein: 5.8g**

CHAPTER 8: SNACKS AND APPETIZERS

FLOURLESS CHOCOLATE HAZELNUT BROWNIE PIE

Prep time: 10 minutes |**Cook time: 30 minutes** |**Serves 8**

- ¾ cup granulated erythritol sweetener
- 4 ounces unsweetened baking chocolate, coarsely chopped
- 4 large eggs, room temperature
- ½ cup boiling water
- 1 teaspoon pure vanilla extract
- 1 cup hazelnut flour (ground hazelnuts)
- ½ cup (1 stick) unsalted butter
- Optional toppings: whipped heavy cream, toasted hazelnuts

1. Preheat oven to 350°F. Grease a 9-inch glass or ceramic pie dish.
2. In a food processor, pulse erythritol and chopped chocolate until finely ground. With processor running, carefully pour in boiling water and process until chocolate is melted and smooth.
3. Add vanilla, butter, and eggs. Process until well combined. Add hazelnut flour and pulse until incorporated.
4. Pour batter into prepared pie dish. Bake 25-30 minutes, or until edges are set but center is still slightly fudgy.
5. Cool completely, then refrigerate for 2 hours before serving.
6. If desired, garnish with whipped cream and toasted hazelnuts.

Per Serving

Calories: 324 |**Fat: 28.4g** | **Carbs: 6.8g** |**Protein: 7.3g** | **Fiber: 3.9g**

VEGGIE BITES

Prep time: 5 minutes | **Cook time: 30 minutes** |**Serves 3**

- ½ cup cream cheese, softened
- ¼ cup mayonnaise
- 1 teaspoon Dijon mustard
- 1 large cucumber, sliced into ¼-inch rounds
- 1 large bell pepper, cut into wide strips
- 1 teaspoon paprika
- Fresh herbs for garnish (optional)

1. In a medium bowl, beat cream cheese until smooth. Add mayonnaise and Dijon mustard; mix until well combined.
2. Arrange cucumber rounds and pepper strips on a serving platter.
3. Top each vegetable piece with a dollop of the cheese mixture using a small spoon or piping bag.
4. Sprinkle with paprika and garnish with fresh herbs if desired.
5. Refrigerate for at least 30 minutes before serving.

Per Serving

Calories: 164 | **Fat: 16.3g** | **Carbs: 3g** | **Protein: 2g** | **Fiber: 0.6g**

CRUSTLESS COCONUT CUSTARD PIE

Prep time: **10 minutes** | Cook time: **50 minutes** | Serves **8**

- 1 cup heavy whipping cream
- ¾ cup powdered erythritol sweetener
- ½ cup full-fat canned coconut milk
- 4 large eggs, room temperature
- ¼ cup (½ stick) unsalted butter, melted and cooled
- 1¼ cups unsweetened shredded coconut
- 3 tablespoons coconut flour
- ½ teaspoon baking powder
- ½ teaspoon pure vanilla extract
- ¼ teaspoon salt

1. Preheat oven to 350°F. Grease a 9-inch glass or ceramic pie dish.
2. In a blender, combine melted butter, eggs, coconut milk, sweetener, and cream. Blend until smooth.
3. Add vanilla, baking powder, salt, coconut flour, and 1 cup shredded coconut. Blend until well combined.
4. Pour mixture into prepared pie dish. Sprinkle remaining ¼ cup coconut over top.
5. Bake 40-50 minutes, or until edges are set but center is still slightly jiggly.
6. Cool for 30 minutes at room temperature, then refrigerate for 2 hours before serving.

Per Serving

Calories: **477** | Fat: **29.5g** | Carbs: **6.7g** | Protein: **5.3g** | Fiber: **2.6g**

CONFETTI CUPCAKES

Prep time: **20 minutes** | Cook time: **30 minutes** | Serves **12**

- 2½ cups blanched almond flour
- ¾ cup granulated erythritol sweetener
- ¼ cup unflavored whey protein powder
- 2 teaspoons baking powder
- ¼ teaspoon salt
- ½ cup full-fat sour cream or Greek yogurt, room temperature
- 4 large egg whites, room temperature
- ¾ teaspoon pure vanilla extract
- 1 tablespoon sugar-free sprinkles, plus more for decorating
- 1 recipe keto Swiss meringue buttercream frosting

1. Preheat oven to 325°F. Line a standard 12-cup muffin pan with silicone or paper liners.
2. In a large bowl, whisk together almond flour, erythritol, protein powder, baking powder, and salt.
3. Add sour cream, egg whites, and vanilla to the dry ingredients. Mix until well combined.
4. Gently fold in sugar-free sprinkles, being careful not to overmix to prevent color bleeding.
5. Divide batter evenly among prepared muffin cups, filling each about ¾ full.
6. Bake for 25-30 minutes, or until tops are lightly golden and spring back when lightly pressed.
7. Cool completely in pan on a wire rack before frosting.
8. Once cooled, frost cupcakes with prepared keto Swiss meringue buttercream.
9. Garnish with additional sugar-free sprinkles if desired.

Per Serving

Calories: **289** | Fat: **24.4g** | Carbs: **5.9g** | Fiber: **2.5g** | Protein: **8.8g**

FRESH BERRY MASCARPONE TART

Prep time: **30 minutes** | Cook time: **20 minutes** | Serves **10**

For the Filling:
- 8 ounces mascarpone cheese, softened
- 4 ounces cream cheese, softened
- 6 tablespoons powdered erythritol sweetener
- ¼ cup heavy whipping cream, room temperature
- 1 teaspoon fresh lemon zest, plus extra for garnish
- 1 teaspoon pure vanilla extract

For the Topping:
- ½ cup fresh raspberries
- ½ cup fresh blueberries
- ½ cup fresh strawberries, sliced
- Thin strips of lemon zest, for garnish

Plus:
- 1 prepared keto coconut flour pie crust

1. Preheat oven to 350°F. Grease a 9-inch tart pan with removable bottom.
2. Prepare and pre-bake coconut flour crust according to recipe directions. Pierce bottom with fork before baking.
3. Bake crust for 20 minutes, or until edges are golden and center is firm. Cool completely.
4. In a large bowl using an electric mixer, beat mascarpone and cream cheese until smooth.
5. Add powdered sweetener, heavy cream, lemon zest, and vanilla. Beat until well combined and creamy.
6. Spread filling evenly in cooled crust.
7. Arrange fresh berries decoratively over filling.
8. Garnish with lemon zest strips.
9. Refrigerate for at least 30 minutes before serving.
10. Store covered in refrigerator for up to 3 days.

Per Serving

Calories: **285** | Fat: **21.2g** | Carbs: **7.6g** | Fiber: **3.3g** | Protein: **5g**

COCONUT FAT BOMBS

Prep time: **10 minutes** | Cook time: **10 minutes** | Serves **8**

- ½ cup unsweetened shredded coconut
- ¼ cup coconut oil, melted
- 2 tablespoons almond butter
- 2 tablespoons granulated erythritol
- 1 teaspoon pure vanilla extract

1. In a medium bowl, combine shredded coconut, melted coconut oil, almond butter, erythritol, and vanilla extract. Stir until well combined.
2. Using a small cookie scoop or spoon, divide mixture evenly among 8 cavities of a silicone mold or mini muffin tin.
3. Place in freezer for at least 30 minutes or until completely firm.
4. Pop fat bombs out of molds and transfer to an airtight container. Store in refrigerator for up to 2 weeks.

Per Serving

Calories: **160** | Fat: **14g** | Carbs: **4g** | Fiber: **2g** | Protein: **2g**

HOT ARTICHOKE AND CHEESE DIP

Prep time: 5 minutes | Cook time: 25 minutes |Serves 10

- 2 (14-ounce) cans artichoke hearts, drained and roughly chopped
- 8 ounces cream cheese, softened
- ½ cup plain Greek yogurt
- ½ cup mayonnaise
- 2 cloves garlic, minced
- 5 cups (20 ounces) Monterey Jack cheese, shredded, divided
- Salt and freshly ground black pepper, to taste
- Celery sticks, cucumber rounds, or low-carb crackers for serving

1. Preheat oven to 350°F. Lightly grease a 2-quart baking dish.
2. In a large bowl, combine artichoke hearts, cream cheese, Greek yogurt, mayonnaise, garlic, and 3 cups of the shredded cheese. Mix well.
3. Season with salt and pepper to taste.
4. Transfer mixture to prepared baking dish. Top with remaining 2 cups cheese.
5. Bake for 20-25 minutes, or until bubbly and lightly golden on top.
6. Let rest for 5 minutes before serving with vegetables or low-carb crackers.

Per Serving

Calories: 367 | Fat: 31.7g | Carbs: 5.1g | Fiber: 2.4g | Protein: 16.2g

CREAM CHEESE BISCUITS

Prep time: 15 minutes |Cook time: 15 minutes |Serves 10

- 1¾ cups blanched almond flour, plus more for dusting
- ¼ cup unflavored egg white protein powder
- 1 tablespoon baking powder
- ½ teaspoon salt
- ½ teaspoon garlic powder (optional)
- 6 ounces cream cheese, cold and cubed
- 1 large egg, room temperature
- ¼ cup unsalted butter, cold and cubed
- 2 tablespoons heavy cream (optional for added richness)

1. Preheat oven to 350°F. Line a baking sheet with parchment paper or a silicone baking mat.
2. In a food processor, combine almond flour, protein powder, baking powder, salt, and garlic powder (if using). Pulse several times to combine.
3. Add cold cream cheese cubes and butter. Pulse until mixture resembles coarse crumbs, about 8-10 pulses.
4. Transfer mixture to a large bowl. Add egg and heavy cream (if using) and mix with a fork until dough comes together.
5. Turn dough onto a lightly almond-floured surface. Gently knead 2-3 times until smooth, adding more flour if needed to prevent sticking.
6. Shape dough into a 10-inch log. Cut into 10 equal slices (about 1-inch thick).
7. Place biscuits on prepared baking sheet, spacing 2 inches apart.
8. Bake for 15 minutes, or until golden brown and firm to the touch.
9. Cool on the baking sheet for at least 15 minutes before serving.

Per Serving

Calories: 355 | Fat: 24g | Carbs: 5.6g | Fiber: 2.1g | Protein: 7.6g

BASIC ALMOND FLOUR MUFFINS

Prep time: 12 minutes | **Cook time: 25 minutes** | **Serves 12**

- 2½ cups blanched almond flour
- ⅓ cup granulated erythritol or monk fruit sweetener
- ¼ cup unflavored whey protein powder
- 2 teaspoons baking powder
- ¼ teaspoon salt
- 3 large eggs, room temperature
- ½ cup (1 stick) unsalted butter, melted and slightly cooled
- ½ cup unsweetened almond milk, room temperature
- ½ teaspoon pure vanilla extract

1. Preheat oven to 325°F. Line a standard 12-cup muffin pan with silicone or paper liners.
2. In a large bowl, whisk together almond flour, sweetener, protein powder, baking powder, and salt until well combined.
3. In a separate bowl, whisk together eggs, melted butter, almond milk, and vanilla extract.
4. Add wet ingredients to dry ingredients and stir until just combined. Don't overmix.
5. Divide batter evenly among prepared muffin cups, filling each about 2/3 full.
6. Bake for 20-25 minutes, or until tops are golden brown and a toothpick inserted into the center comes out clean.
7. Let cool in pan for 5 minutes, then transfer to a wire rack to cool completely.

Per Serving

Calories: **329** | Fat: **20.1g** | Carbs: **5.5g** | Fiber: **2.5g** | Protein: **8.1g**

CHOCOLATE ALMOND KETO COOKIES

Prep time: 10 minutes | **Cook time: 25 minutes** | **Serves 10**

- ½ cup ghee or unsalted butter, melted
- ¼ cup almonds, finely chopped
- 1 tablespoon unsweetened cocoa powder
- 1 cup almond flour
- 1 cup unsweetened almond milk
- ½ teaspoon pure vanilla extract
- 1 teaspoon baking powder
- 2 tablespoons granulated stevia sweetener
- 3 large eggs, beaten

1. Preheat oven to 360°F. Line a baking sheet with parchment paper.
2. In a large bowl, whisk together all ingredients until well combined.
3. Drop rounded tablespoons of batter onto prepared baking sheet, spacing cookies 2 inches apart. Gently flatten each cookie.
4. Bake for 25 minutes, or until edges are lightly golden.
5. Let cool completely on baking sheet before serving.

Per Serving

Calories: **450** | Fat: **34g** | Fiber: **7g** | Carbs: **10g** | Protein: **20g**

BACON-WRAPPED SHRIMP

Prep time: **5 minutes** | Cook time:**15 minutes** |Serves **8**

- 24 medium shrimp, peeled and deveined
- 8 slices thick-cut bacon, cut crosswise into thirds
- 1 teaspoon dry mustard powder
- 1 teaspoon onion powder
- ½ teaspoon garlic powder
- ½ teaspoon crushed red pepper flakes
- Kosher salt and freshly ground black pepper, to taste

1. Preheat oven to 400°F. Line a large rimmed baking sheet with foil or a silicone baking mat.
2. Pat shrimp dry with paper towels. Wrap each shrimp with a piece of bacon, securing with a toothpick.
3. Arrange wrapped shrimp on prepared baking sheet, leaving space between each piece.
4. In a small bowl, combine mustard powder, onion powder, garlic powder, and red pepper flakes.
5. Sprinkle seasoning mixture evenly over shrimp. Season with salt and black pepper.
6. Bake for 12-15 minutes, or until shrimp are pink and bacon is crispy.
7. Let rest for 2-3 minutes before serving.

Per Serving

Calories: **119** | Fat: **10.3g** | Carbs: **0.3g** | Protein: **5.7g** | Fiber: **0g**

PEANUT BUTTER CARAMEL COOKIES

Prep time: **5 minutes** |Cook time: **10 minutes** |Serves **8**

- ¾ cup creamy peanut butter (no sugar added)
- 1 cup sugar-free caramel sauce
- ½ teaspoon vanilla extract or caramel extract
- ¾ cup sliced almonds
- ¾ cup unsweetened coconut flakes
- ¼ cup powdered erythritol sweetener
- 3 ounces pork rinds, finely crushed

1. Line a baking sheet with parchment paper.
2. In a medium saucepan over low heat, combine peanut butter and caramel sauce. Stir until smooth and well combined. Remove from heat and stir in extract.
3. In a food processor, pulse almonds and coconut flakes until mixture resembles the texture of oatmeal.
4. Add the almond-coconut mixture, sweetener, and crushed pork rinds to the peanut butter mixture. Stir until well combined.
5. Drop rounded tablespoons of mixture onto prepared baking sheet, spacing cookies 2 inches apart. Gently flatten each cookie with your palm.
6. Refrigerate for 1 hour or until firm.

Per Serving

Calories: **316**| Fat: **16.6g** | Carbs: **5.1g** | Protein: **7.3g** | Fiber: **1.7g**

CHAPTER 9: DESSERTS AND DRINKS

RHUBARB MUG CAKES

Prep time: 5 minutes | Cook time: 2 minutes | Serves 2

- 1 large egg, room temperature
- 3 tablespoons refined avocado oil or macadamia nut oil
- 4 teaspoons powdered erythritol sweetener
- ¼ teaspoon pure vanilla extract
- ¼ cup ground flaxseed
- 1 teaspoon ground cinnamon
- ¼ teaspoon ground nutmeg
- ¼ teaspoon baking powder
- 1 piece fresh rhubarb (2½ inches), finely diced
- Fresh strawberry slices for garnish (optional)

1. In a small bowl, whisk together egg, oil, erythritol, and vanilla until well combined.
2. In another bowl, mix ground flaxseed, cinnamon, nutmeg, and baking powder.
3. Add dry ingredients to wet ingredients, stirring until just combined.
4. Fold in diced rhubarb.
5. Divide batter evenly between two 8-ounce microwave-safe ramekins or mugs.
6. Microwave individually for 2-2½ minutes, or until toothpick inserted in center comes out clean.
7. Let cool for 1 minute before garnishing with strawberry slices if desired.

Per Serving

Calories: **303** | Fat: **27.8g** | Carbs: **7.3g** | Fiber: **5.5g** | Protein: **6g**

CHOCOLATE AVOCADO MOUSSE

Prep time: 10 minutes | Cook time: 30 minutes | Serves 4

- 1 large ripe avocado (about 200g), peeled and pitted
- ¼ cup unsweetened cocoa powder
- 2 tablespoons granulated erythritol sweetener
- ¼ cup heavy cream, cold
- 1 teaspoon pure vanilla extract
- ⅛ teaspoon salt
- Fresh berries for garnish (optional)

1. Cut avocado in half, remove pit, and scoop flesh into food processor or blender.
2. Add cocoa powder, erythritol, heavy cream, vanilla, and salt.
3. Process until completely smooth and creamy, scraping down sides as needed.
4. Divide mousse among 4 serving dishes.
5. Chill for at least 30 minutes before serving.
6. Garnish with fresh berries if desired.

Per Serving

Calories: **210** | Fat: **18g** | Carbs: **6g** | Fiber: **4g** | Protein: **2g**

DAIRY-FREE COCONUT WHIPPED CREAM

Prep time: **5 minutes** | Cook time: **5 minutes** | Serves **7**

- 1 (13.5 oz) can coconut cream OR cream from
- 2 (13.5 oz) cans full-fat coconut milk

Optional Additions:

- 1 tablespoon powdered erythritol sweetener
- 1 teaspoon pure vanilla extract
- 2 tablespoons unsweetened cacao powder (for chocolate version)

1. Refrigerate coconut cream or milk cans for at least 12 hours.
2. If using coconut milk, scoop out only the solid cream from top (save liquid for other uses).
3. Place cold coconut cream in blender or bowl of stand mixer with whisk attachment.
4. For blender method: Start on low speed, gradually increasing to medium. Blend until whipped cream consistency forms (about 30 seconds).
5. For stand mixer method: Whisk on medium-high for 30 seconds until fluffy.
6. For flavored versions: Add sweetener and vanilla (and cacao if making chocolate).
7. Blend or whisk additional 10 seconds until well combined.
8. Use immediately or refrigerate up to 3 days.

Per Serving

Calories: **116** | Fat: **11.6g** |Carbs: **1.9g** | Fiber: **0g** | Protein: **1g**

STRAWBERRY MILKSHAKE

Prep time: **5 minutes** | Cook time: **10 minutes** |Serves **2**

- 6 ounces fresh or frozen strawberries (170g), hulled
- ⅔ cup water
- ½ cup full-fat coconut milk (120ml), frozen into cubes
- ½ teaspoon pure vanilla extract

1. If using frozen strawberries, thaw completely.
2. Add strawberries, water, frozen coconut milk cubes, and vanilla to blender.
3. Blend on high speed for 40-50 seconds until completely smooth.
4. Pour into glasses and serve immediately.

Per Serving

Calories: **121** | Fat: **9.8 g** | Carbs: **7.2 g** | Fiber: **1.7 g** | Protein: **1.1 g**

VANILLA CHIA SEED PUDDING

Prep time: 5 minutes | Cook time: 10 minutes | Serves 2

- ¼ cup chia seeds
- 1 cup unsweetened almond milk
- 1 tablespoon granulated erythritol sweetener
- ½ teaspoon pure vanilla extract
- Fresh berries for topping (optional)
- Keto-friendly granola for topping (optional)

1. In a medium bowl, combine chia seeds, almond milk, erythritol, and vanilla. Whisk well.
2. Let stand 5 minutes, then whisk again to prevent clumping.
3. Cover and refrigerate for at least 4 hours or overnight.
4. Before serving, stir well and check consistency. If too thick, thin with additional almond milk.
5. Top with fresh berries or granola if desired.

Per Serving

Calories: **150** | Fat: **9g** | Carbs: **10g** | Fiber: **8g** | Protein: **4g**

CHOCOLATE CHIP COOKIES

Prep time: 10 minutes | Cook time: 12 minutes | Serves 12

- 1½ cups blanched almond flour
- ¼ cup granulated erythritol sweetener
- ½ teaspoon baking soda
- ¼ teaspoon salt
- ½ cup unsalted butter, softened
- 1 large egg, room temperature
- 1 teaspoon pure vanilla extract
- ¼ cup sugar-free chocolate chips

1. Preheat oven to 350°F. Line a baking sheet with parchment paper.
2. In a medium bowl, whisk together almond flour, erythritol, baking soda, and salt.
3. In a large bowl, cream butter until light and fluffy, about 2 minutes.
4. Beat in egg and vanilla until well combined.
5. Gradually stir dry ingredients into wet ingredients until dough forms.
6. Fold in chocolate chips.
7. Drop rounded tablespoons of dough onto prepared baking sheet, spacing 2 inches apart.
8. Bake 10-12 minutes until edges are golden brown.
9. Cool on baking sheet for 5 minutes, then transfer to wire rack.

Per Serving

Calories: **211** | Fat: **18g** | Carbs: **4g** | Fiber: **2g** | Protein: **5g**

MINI CHEESECAKE BITES

Prep time: **15 minutes** | Cook time: **10 minutes** | Serves **12**

For the Filling:

- 8 ounces cream cheese, softened
- ¼ cup granulated erythritol sweetener
- 1 teaspoon pure vanilla extract

For the Crust:

- ½ cup almond flour
- ¼ cup unsweetened shredded coconut
- 1 tablespoon butter, melted

1. Preheat oven to 350°F. Line a 12-cup mini muffin tin with paper liners.
2. Make the filling: Beat cream cheese, erythritol, and vanilla until smooth and creamy.
3. Make the crust: Combine almond flour, coconut, and melted butter until mixture resembles wet sand.
4. Press crust mixture into bottom of lined muffin cups.
5. Pipe or spoon cream cheese mixture over crusts.
6. Bake 10-12 minutes until edges are lightly golden.
7. Cool completely in pan, then refrigerate 1 hour before serving.

Per Serving

Calories: **180** | Fat: **16g** | Carbs: **3g** | Fiber: **2g** | Protein: **5g**

KETO ICED COFFEE

Prep time: **5 minutes** | Cook time: **0 minutes** | Serves **2**

- 1 cup strong brewed coffee, chilled
- ½ cup unsweetened almond milk
- 1 tablespoon granulated erythritol sweetener
- Ice cubes
- Heavy cream for topping (optional)
- Ground cinnamon for garnish (optional)

1. Brew coffee double strength and chill completely.
2. In a tall glass or mason jar, combine chilled coffee, almond milk, and erythritol.
3. Stir until sweetener dissolves completely.
4. Fill glasses with ice and pour coffee mixture over.
5. Top with a splash of heavy cream and sprinkle of cinnamon if desired.

Per Serving

Calories: **20** | Fat: **1g** | Carbs: **2g** | Fiber: **1g** | Protein: **0g**

SUGAR-FREE LEMONADE

Prep time: **5 minutes** | Cook time: **5 minutes** | Serves **4**

- ½ cup fresh lemon juice (about 3-4 large lemons)
- 3 cups cold filtered water
- 2 tablespoons granulated erythritol sweetener
- Ice cubes
- Lemon slices and fresh mint for garnish (optional)

1. In a pitcher, combine lemon juice, water, and erythritol.
2. Stir until sweetener completely dissolves.
3. Taste and adjust sweetness if needed.
4. Serve over ice, garnished with lemon slices and mint if desired.

Per Serving

Calories: **10** | Fat: **0g** | Carbs: **3g** | Fiber: **0g** | Protein: **0g**

NO-BAKE KETO ENERGY BITES

Prep time: **5 minutes** | Cook time: **10 minutes** |Serves **10**

- ½ cup coconut flour
- ½ cup almond flour
- ¼ cup granulated erythritol
- 2 tablespoons heavy cream or unsweetened almond milk
- ½ cup natural peanut butter, melted
- ¼ teaspoon ground cinnamon
- ¼ teaspoon ground star anise (optional)
- 1 teaspoon pure vanilla extract
- ⅛ teaspoon coarse sea salt
- ¼ cup sugar-free chocolate chips

1. In a large bowl, combine coconut flour, almond flour, erythritol, cream, melted peanut butter, cinnamon, star anise (if using), vanilla, and salt. Mix until smooth and well combined.
2. Fold in chocolate chips.
3. Scoop mixture into a silicone ice cube tray or roll into 1-inch balls.
4. Refrigerate for 1 hour before serving.

Per Serving

Calories: **102** | Fat: **7.8g** | Carbs: **5.8g** | Protein: **2.6g** | Fiber: **1.8g**

CHAPTER 10: BASES, CONDIMENTS AND SAUCES

CREAMY ITALIAN DRESSING

Prep time: **5 minutes** | Cook time:**5 minutes** |Serves **1**

- ¾ cup light-tasting oil, such as avocado oil or light olive oil
- ¼ cup plus 2 tablespoons mayonnaise
- 3 tablespoons red wine vinegar
- 1 tablespoon distilled vinegar
- 1 tablespoon lemon juice
- 1 tablespoon onion powder
- 1½ teaspoons dried basil
- 1½ teaspoons ground black pepper
- ¾ teaspoon garlic powder
- ¾ teaspoon dried oregano leaves
- ¾ teaspoon dried thyme leaves
- ½ teaspoon red pepper flakes
- ¼ teaspoon finely ground sea salt

1. Place all the ingredients in a 16-ounce or larger airtight container. Cover and shake until incorporated.
2. When ready to serve, give the container a little shake and enjoy.

Per Serving

Calories: **86** | Fat: **9.3 g** | Carbs: **0.5 g** | Fiber: **0.1 g** |Protein: **0.1 g**

CAESAR DRESSING

Prep time: **5 minutes** | Cook time: **10 minutes** | Serves **3**

- ½ cup mayonnaise
- 1 tablespoon Dijon mustard
- Juice of ½ lemon
- ½ teaspoon Worcestershire sauce
- Pinch pink Himalayan salt
- Pinch freshly ground black pepper
- ¼ cup grated Parmesan cheese

1. In a medium bowl, whisk together the mayonnaise, mustard, lemon juice, Worcestershire sauce, pink Himalayan salt, and pepper until fully combined.
2. Add the Parmesan cheese, and whisk until creamy and well blended.
3. Keep in a sealed glass container in the refrigerator for up to 1 week.

Per Serving

Calories: **222** | Fat: **23g** | Carbs: **2g** | Fiber: **0g** | Protein: **2g**

RANCH DRESSING

Prep time: **5 minutes** | Cook time: **0 minutes** | Serves **8**

- ½ cup sour cream
- ¼ cup mayonnaise
- 1 tablespoon fresh dill, chopped
- 1 tablespoon fresh chives, chopped
- ½ teaspoon garlic powder
- ¼ teaspoon onion powder
- 1 tablespoon lemon juice
- Salt and pepper to taste

1. In a mixing bowl, combine the sour cream, mayonnaise, dill, chives, garlic powder, onion powder, and lemon juice.
2. Stir until well combined and season with salt and pepper to taste.
3. Refrigerate for at least 30 minutes to allow flavors to meld before serving.

Per Serving

Calories: **100** | Fat: **10g** | Carbs: **1g** | Fiber: **0g** | Protein: **1g**

KETO MAYONNAISE

Prep time: **5 minutes** | Cook time: **0 minutes** | Serves **12**

- 1 large egg (room temperature)
- 1 tablespoon Dijon mustard
- 1 tablespoon lemon juice
- 1 cup avocado oil
- ¼ teaspoon sea salt
- Pinch of white pepper

1. In a tall jar or mixing bowl, combine the egg, mustard, lemon juice, salt, and pepper.
2. Using an immersion blender, blend the mixture until smooth, about 20–30 seconds.
3. With the blender running, slowly drizzle in the avocado oil until the mixture thickens to your desired consistency.
4. Store in an airtight container in the fridge for up to a week.

Per Serving

Calories: **120** | Fat: **13g** | Carbs: **0g** | Fiber: **0g** | Protein: **1g**

PESTO SAUCE

Prep time: **10 minutes** | Cook time: **0 minutes** | Serves **8**

- 2 cups fresh basil leaves
- ¼ cup grated Parmesan cheese
- ¼ cup pine nuts (or walnuts)
- 2 cloves garlic
- ½ cup olive oil
- Salt and pepper to taste

1. In a food processor, combine the basil, Parmesan cheese, pine nuts, and garlic.
2. Pulse until finely chopped, then slowly stream in the olive oil while the processor is running until a smooth paste forms.
3. Season with salt and pepper to taste.
4. Store in an airtight container in the fridge for up to a week.

Per Serving

Calories: **150** | Fat: **14g** | Carbs: **3g** | Fiber: **1g** | Protein: **4g**

BBQ SAUCE

Prep time: **5 minutes** | Cook time: **15 minutes** | Serves **8**

- 1 cup sugar-free ketchup
- 2 tablespoons apple cider vinegar
- 1 tablespoon Worcestershire sauce
- 1 tablespoon mustard
- 1 tablespoon erythritol (or sweetener of choice)
- ¼ teaspoon smoked paprika
- ¼ teaspoon garlic powder
- ¼ teaspoon onion powder
- Salt and pepper to taste

1. In a saucepan over medium heat, combine the ketchup, apple cider vinegar, Worcestershire sauce, mustard, erythritol, smoked paprika, garlic powder, and onion powder.
2. Bring to a simmer and cook for 10–15 minutes, stirring occasionally, until thickened.
3. Season with salt and pepper to taste and let cool before serving.

Per Serving

Calories: **40** | Fat: **0g** | Carbs: **3g** | Fiber: **1g** | Protein: **1g**

ALFREDO SAUCE

Prep time: **5 minutes** | Cook time: **10 minutes** | Serves **4**

- ½ cup unsalted butter
- 1 cup heavy cream
- 1 cup grated Parmesan cheese
- ½ teaspoon garlic powder
- Salt and pepper to taste

1. In a saucepan, melt the butter over medium heat.
2. Add the heavy cream and bring to a simmer. Cook for 2-3 minutes until it thickens slightly.
3. Stir in the Parmesan cheese and garlic powder, and cook for another 2–3 minutes until the sauce is smooth.
4. Season with salt and pepper to taste.

Per Serving

Calories: **270** | Fat: **26g** | Carbs: **3g** | Fiber: **0g** | Protein: **7g**

TOMATO SAUCE

Prep time: **5 minutes** | Cook time: **20 minutes** | Serves **6**

- 1 can (14 oz) crushed tomatoes
- 1 tablespoon olive oil
- ½ teaspoon garlic powder
- 1 teaspoon dried oregano
- ¼ teaspoon onion powder
- Salt and pepper to taste
- Fresh basil for garnish

1. In a saucepan, heat the olive oil over medium heat.
2. Add the garlic powder, oregano, and onion powder. Cook for 1 minute to release the flavors.
3. Stir in the crushed tomatoes and bring to a simmer.
4. Cook for 15–20 minutes, stirring occasionally, until the sauce thickens.
5. Season with salt and pepper, and garnish with fresh basil before serving.

Per Serving

Calories: **60** | Fat: **4g** | Carbs: **6g** | Fiber: **2g** | Protein: **2g**

HONEY MUSTARD DRESSING & MARINADE

Prep time: 5 minutes | Cook time:5 minutes |Serves 1

- 1 cup light-tasting oil, such as avocado oil or light olive oil
- ¼ cup apple cider vinegar
- ¼ cup Dijon mustard
- 2 tablespoons lemon juice
- 1 tablespoon plus 1 teaspoon honey
- ½ teaspoon finely ground sea salt

1. Place all the ingredients in an 18-ounce or larger airtight container. Cover and shake until incorporated.
2. When ready to serve, give the container a little shake and enjoy.

Per Serving

Calories: **74** | Fat: **7.9 g** | Carbs: **1 g** | Fiber: **0.1 g** |Protein: **0.1 g**

TZATZIKI SAUCE

Prep time: 10 minutes | Cook time: 0 minutes | Serves 6

- 1 cup Greek yogurt (full-fat, unsweetened)
- ½ cucumber, grated and excess water squeezed out
- 1 tablespoon olive oil
- 1 tablespoon fresh dill, chopped
- 1 clove garlic, minced
- 1 tablespoon lemon juice
- Salt and pepper to taste

1. In a mixing bowl, combine the Greek yogurt, grated cucumber, olive oil, dill, garlic, and lemon juice.
2. Stir until well combined, and season with salt and pepper to taste.
3. Chill for at least 30 minutes before serving.

Per Serving

Calories: **60** | Fat: **5g** | Carbs: **3g** | Fiber: **1g** | Protein: **3g**

CREAMY MUSTARD SAUCE

Prep time: 5 minutes | Cook time: 5 minutes | Serves 4

- ¼ cup Dijon mustard
- ¼ cup mayonnaise
- 2 tablespoons heavy cream
- 1 tablespoon apple cider vinegar
- 1 teaspoon fresh dill, chopped
- Salt and pepper to taste

1. In a bowl, whisk together the Dijon mustard, mayonnaise, heavy cream, and apple cider vinegar.
2. Stir in the fresh dill and season with salt and pepper to taste.
3. Serve immediately or refrigerate for up to a week.

Per Serving

Calories: **90** | Fat: **9g** | Carbs: **1g** | Fiber: **0g** | Protein: **1g**

GARLIC BUTTER SAUCE

Prep time: 5 minutes | Cook time: 5 minutes | Serves 4

- ½ cup unsalted butter
- 4 cloves garlic, minced
- 1 tablespoon fresh parsley, chopped
- Salt and pepper to taste

1. In a saucepan, melt the butter over medium heat.
2. Add the minced garlic and cook for 1–2 minutes until fragrant, stirring constantly.
3. Remove from heat and stir in the fresh parsley, salt, and pepper.
4. Serve immediately over your favorite protein or vegetables.

Per Serving

Calories: **140** | Fat: **14g** | Carbs: **1g** | Fiber: **0g** | Protein: **1g**

APPENDIX 1: MEASUREMENT CONVERSION CHART

MEASUREMENT CONVERSION CHART

VOLUME EQUIVALENTS(DRY)

US STANDARD	METRIC (APPROXIMATE)
1/8 teaspoon	0.5 mL
1/4 teaspoon	1 mL
1/2 teaspoon	2 mL
3/4 teaspoon	4 mL
1 teaspoon	5 mL
1 tablespoon	15 mL
1/4 cup	59 mL
1/2 cup	118 mL
3/4 cup	177 mL
1 cup	235 mL
2 cups	475 mL
3 cups	700 mL
4 cups	1 L

VOLUME EQUIVALENTS(LIQUID)

US STANDARD	US STANDARD (OUNCES)	METRIC (APPROXIMATE)
2 tablespoons	1 fl.oz.	30 mL
1/4 cup	2 fl.oz.	60 mL
1/2 cup	4 fl.oz.	120 mL
1 cup	8 fl.oz.	240 mL
1 1/2 cup	12 fl.oz.	355 mL
2 cups or 1 pint	16 fl.oz.	475 mL
4 cups or 1 quart	32 fl.oz.	1 L
1 gallon	128 fl.oz.	4 L

TEMPERATURES EQUIVALENTS

FAHRENHEIT(F)	CELSIUS(C) (APPROXIMATE)
225 °F	107 °C
250 °F	120 °C
275 °F	135 °C
300 °F	150 °C
325 °F	160 °C
350 °F	180 °C
375 °F	190 °C
400 °F	205 °C
425 °F	220 °C
450 °F	235 °C
475 °F	245 °C
500 °F	260 °C

WEIGHT EQUIVALENTS

US STANDARD	METRIC (APPROXIMATE)
1 ounce	28 g
2 ounces	57 g
5 ounces	142 g
10 ounces	284 g
15 ounces	425 g
16 ounces (1 pound)	455 g
1.5 pounds	680 g
2 pounds	907 g

The Dirty Dozen and Clean Fifteen

The Environmental Working Group (EWG) is a nonprofit, nonpartisan organization dedicated to protecting human health and the environment Its mission is to empower people to live healthier lives in a healthier environment. This organization publishes an annual list of the twelve kinds of produce, in sequence, that have the highest amount of pesticide residue-the Dirty Dozen-as well as a list of the fifteen kinds of produce that have the least amount of pesticide residue-the Clean Fifteen.

THE DIRTY DOZEN	THE CLEAN FIFTEEN
• The 2016 Dirty Dozen includes the following produce. These are considered among the year's most important produce to buy organic:	• The least critical to buy organically are the Clean Fifteen list. The following are on the 2016 list:

THE DIRTY DOZEN

Strawberries	Spinach
Apples	Tomatoes
Nectarines	Bell peppers
Peaches	Cherry tomatoes
Celery	Cucumbers
Grapes	Kale/collard greens
Cherries	Hot peppers

THE CLEAN FIFTEEN

Avocados	Papayas
Corn	Kiw
Pineapples	Eggplant
Cabbage	Honeydew
Sweet peas	Grapefruit
Onions	Cantaloupe
Asparagus	Cauliflower
Mangos	

• *The Dirty Dozen list contains two additional itemskale/collard greens and hot peppers-because they tend to contain trace levels of highly hazardous pesticides.*

• *Some of the sweet corn sold in the United States are made from genetically engineered (GE) seedstock. Buy organic varieties of these crops to avoid GE produce.*

Hey there!

Wow, can you believe we've reached the end of this culinary journey together? I'm truly thrilled and filled with joy as I think back on all the recipes we've shared and the flavors we've discovered. This experience, blending a bit of tradition with our own unique twists, has been a journey of love for good food. And knowing you've been out there, giving these dishes a try, has made this adventure incredibly special to me.

Even though we're turning the last page of this book, I hope our conversation about all things delicious doesn't have to end. I cherish your thoughts, your experiments, and yes, even those moments when things didn't go as planned. Every piece of feedback you share is invaluable, helping to enrich this experience for us all.

I'd be so grateful if you could take a moment to share your thoughts with me, be it through a review on Amazon or any other place you feel comfortable expressing yourself online. Whether it's praise, constructive criticism, or even an idea for how we might do things differently in the future, your input is what truly makes this journey meaningful.

This book is a piece of my heart, offered to you with all the love and enthusiasm I have for cooking. But it's your engagement and your words that elevate it to something truly extraordinary.

Thank you from the bottom of my heart for being such an integral part of this culinary adventure. Your openness to trying new things and sharing your experiences has been the greatest gift.

Catch you later,

Christina J. Williamson

Printed in Great Britain
by Amazon

57927067R00044